CODE HALOS

How the Digital Lives
of People, Things, and Organizations
Are Changing the Rules of Business

A Playbook for Managers

Malcolm Frank
Paul Roehrig
Benjamin Pring

WILEY

Contents

Acknowledgments

In our work leading Cognizant's Center for the Future of Work, our goal is to help our clients understand and leverage new technologies that will improve their businesses. In doing so, we collaborate extensively with a wide range of business and technology leaders, academics, and industry thought leaders. In particular, we'd like to thank our clients. There are too many to list here, but we are continually challenged and inspired by their insight and drive to create more successful businesses. Leading academics have also helped shape our ideas. In particular we'd like to thank Andy McAfee of MIT, Jonathan Zittrain of Harvard, Ramayya Krishnan from CMU, and Soumitra Dutta from Cornell. We are profoundly grateful for guidance from many business and technology thought leaders. Geoffrey Moore, Thornton May, Juan Enriquez, Bruce Rogow, Vinnie Mirchandani, Tom Davenport, DJ Patil, and Don Tapscott have all helped us strengthen our ideas.

Richard Narramore, Tiffany Colon, Christine Moore, and Peter Knox from Wiley have helped us develop our ideas into this book. Mark Baven, Mary Brandel, and Diana Fitter worked tirelessly to improve and tighten the manuscript. We'd also like to thank Gareth Evans, Matt Gould, Sam Hughes, and the team at Webfire for helping make the book (and the accompanying app) beautiful. Mara Stefan and Emerge PR have helped us connect our ideas to the wider market.

Francisco D'Souza, CEO of Cognizant, has been instrumental in supporting our research and work with customers around Code Halo ideas. Rajendra Mittal, Alan Alper, Euan Davis, Meenu Sharma, Lee Saber, and Zacharyah Abend have all made tremendous contributions to this book. This book is also extensively informed by the many Cognizant associates who are on the front lines of helping hundreds of companies around the world on a daily basis.

Finally, we would like to thank our families for their love, support, and patience during the process of writing this book. Our "day jobs" of consulting to, and working with, some of the world's most important companies come with their own significant demands of time and travel. With the incremental demands of writing a book, the three of us feel remarkably fortunate for the inspiration and encouragement our families provided. We will always feel both thankful and blessed.

Malcolm Frank, Paul Roehrig, Ben Pring
New York, Washington DC, Boston
April 2014

INTRODUCTION

The Value of the Virtual

You probably have a few questions as you check out the title and dive into this book: *What is it really about? Is it any good? Is it relevant to me? Will it help me succeed? Who else is reading it? Who are these three authors, and why should I take them seriously?*

In the past, you would have had to do some due diligence in order to answer those questions: read some reviews, leaf through the book, and also talk to your friends and colleagues to discover their views: *What did you think of the book? Has it helped you? Do you think I should invest my time in reading it?*

Traditionally, that's what you would have had to do. But what if you could answer those questions in less than a minute? Better yet, what if you could get the answers *before you even asked?*

You could, if you harnessed the power of the fields of information that we call **Code Halos**. They surround you, this book, your friends and colleagues, the publisher, and other books in the genre. The book is a physical object of paper and ink and glue (or contained within a physical product such as a tablet or e-reader) that has a Code Halo of virtual information surrounding it: reviews, sales information, the number of your peers who are reading it, LinkedIn profiles of the authors, and more. Similarly, you—the reader—have your own rich and unique digital fingerprint made up of your personal likes and dislikes, your tastes in literature and other forms of entertainment, your current job responsibilities, your network of friends and work colleagues, and your personal preferences for consuming business ideas. If you could connect the information about yourself and this book, you would know—before you even started reading—whether you'd enjoy it and if the content has meaning to you.

The "halo" in the term Code Halo refers to the data that accumulates around people, devices, and organizations—data that's robust, powerful, and continually growing in richness and complexity. The halos contain the *code* that companies, brands, employers, and partners can use to enhance their understanding of people or objects more deeply. Decoding the information within that invisible field, teasing out the insights, and creating new commercial models does not happen automatically or easily. But every employee, product, building, and organization should have a Code Halo, and this book is going to explain how and why.

The halos contain the code that companies, brands, employers, and partners can use to enhance their understanding of people or objects.

While technology makes Code Halos possible, they transcend constructs like IT or Big Data or analytics. Code Halos make meaningful connections between people, organizations, and devices in a business context. Extracting meaning from Code Halos—and applying that understanding to business strategies and practices—is a new and essential yet not clearly or widely understood management skill. This book's purpose is to provide a fact-based understanding of the Code Halo phenomenon and outline a practical approach to improving performance by harnessing their power.

The Emerging Code Halo Economy

We find ourselves in a unique period in the history of commerce, more significant than any we have experienced in our careers. Traditional methods of production have stagnated, while virtual means are growing exponentially. We have already seen Code Halo ideas operating at the heart of the rapid rise of eBusiness superstars such as Google, Amazon, Facebook, and Twitter.

Today's Code Halo leaders go far beyond transactional relationships; they forge deep human connections and even create moments of magic. It can occasionally feel as if these companies are reading your mind as they anticipate needs and fulfill desires you may not have even recognized yourself. *That was my favorite song in college! I've never heard of this author, but she sounds fantastic!*

Nowadays, a growing number of more traditional companies are joining Silicon Valley eBusiness leaders in harnessing the power of Code Halos. General Electric is creating tremendous economic value and richer customer connections by harnessing Code Halos to build what it calls Brilliant Machines. Nike is embracing Code Halos through its Nike+ FuelBand initiative. Disney has introduced the MagicBand to transform the amusement park experience. Allstate is remaking auto insurance with its Drivewise initiative.

You can join the competition or, like another group of companies in industries that have already been disrupted—including Borders, Blockbuster, and Kodak—you can take the risk of suffering what we call an Extinction Event—where a company goes out of business altogether—by ignoring the significance of this transition.

The Crossroads Model of Competition

To compete in this new world, it is necessary for managers to understand how the Code Halo economy works. To that end, we at Cognizant's Center for the Future of Work have researched and consulted to hundreds of the 2,000 largest global companies across dozens of industries, probing their leaders' views. Our findings are fascinating: once Code Halos mature, they impact industry structures in a consistent and violent pattern that we call the **Crossroads Model**. There are four phases of the model, and what companies do—or do not do—with Code Halos in each phase determines their fortunes when they inevitably reach a crossroads. While one route can lead to new levels of market prosperity, the other can take them down a path toward extinction.

Once you recognize the pattern, you see clearly that Amazon eliminating Borders was not a "book thing," nor was Apple outrunning Nokia and BlackBerry a "mobile phone thing," nor was Netflix knocking off Blockbuster a "movie rental thing." Rather, every one of these industries' disruptions was a "Code Halo thing."

Know the Rules

In Part I of this book (Chapters 1 through 7), we'll provide detail on what Code Halos are, the anatomy of an optimal solution, the business models they follow, and the real-world economics of information.

Defining the Crossroads Model is vital to recognizing what's going on within your company and industry. But it's even more important to gain an understanding of the management skills required to master the model. To that end, Part II (Chapters 8 through 11) offers a set of four principles that lie at the heart of success. We'll explain each principle and provide tactical, action-oriented guidance on how your organization can embrace Code Halos.

In Part III (Chapters 12 through 14), we'll provide specific recommendations on how your organization can successfully navigate the Crossroads Model.

Why We Wrote *Code Halos*

We didn't initially set out to write a book on Code Halos. In our roles running Cognizant's Center for the Future of Work, we have the privilege of helping hundreds of clients create business advantage with the new technologies available. While doing this work, we saw a pattern emerge. The more we looked at it, the more obvious it became that it was simply too significant to ignore. So we committed to the nontrivial process of writing this book to share our data and conclusions.

Over the past five years, we've been helping clients manage two sea changes in parallel:

- First, in a post-credit crisis, fully globalized world, it became clear our clients were facing **significant secular business shifts in their industries**. Whether in banking, manufacturing, retail, media, insurance, healthcare, or government, they've recognized quite clearly—albeit with some resulting confusion—that the old rules of business no longer apply.
- Second, as if that wasn't difficult enough, there was a **similar secular shift in technology** under way, as well. The consumer

technology experience—of mobility and social computing—has entered the corporation at a rapid rate, fundamentally changing customers' and employees' technology expectations—and the role of the IT organization itself.

These dual secular shifts created a lot of confusion and noise in the market from around 2008 until now. While many organizations were attempting to harness the power of new consumer technologies like social, mobile, and cloud-enabled solutions in a business setting, only a few were truly succeeding. When we took a closer look at the ones that *were* succeeding, we noticed how they leveraged these new technology capabilities to power through the new business challenges. It was as if the constraints of a tough economy didn't apply to them.

As we investigated this further, two patterns started to emerge.

- First, we saw that the Code Halo acted as the atomic building block for the successful commercialization of consumer technologies.
- Second, companies that implemented Code Halos at scale were driving outsized performance in a very consistent manner, regardless of industry.

We eventually concluded—based on years of experience and a mountain of data—that something immense is happening. Companies that had been successful in the past were either adapting quickly or getting into real trouble.

The three of us have decades of combined experience helping some of the world's leading consulting, advisory, and technology product companies generate business value from technology. We've witnessed from the trenches and high command some of the major shifts in corporate technology: the advent of PCs, enterprise applications, Client/Server architectures, the Internet, and global IT delivery. We have practical experience recognizing business and technology trends, and then helping clients innovate and succeed regardless of their maturity and market position. Yet it became clear to us that the Code Halo movement was something much larger than anything we'd seen before.

The more we tested our ideas, the more excited we became that we were building a language to describe a dynamic that many people are feeling. We deduced a pattern of how this shift takes place that has already played out in many industry sectors. Once we had the right lens—the idea of Code Halos and the Crossroads Model—many elements of ongoing business-technology transformation started making much more sense. We wanted to share our findings and ideas with enterprise executives, leaders in mid-sized companies, investors seeking to fund the next big thing, entrepreneurs trying to create the next big thing, and students building skills to compete in a global economy. We hoped to contribute to better business and stronger economies. The result of that exploration is the book you now have.

Whether you're a product manager, head of a marketing department, running a small business, head of information technology, leading a government agency, or directing your company's strategy, it's essential to understand how much this massive shift pertains to you.

Before we plunge in, a word of caution: some decision-makers view Code Halos as "a CIO issue." Others focus so intensely on the demands of hitting sales targets that they are unable to look ahead and see the Crossroads moment that is surely coming. Either perspective will make you miss an incredible opportunity.

Code Halos are *everybody's* issue. Whether you're a product manager, head of a marketing department, running a small business, head of information technology, leading a government agency, or directing your company's strategy, it's essential to understand how much this massive shift pertains to you. The fundamental basis for value creation is changing right this moment. People—both inside and outside your organization's boundaries—want to engage with you in ways that are dramatically different than ever before. Their expectations for interacting, transacting, communicating, and collaborating with you are shifting rapidly.

The skills for building and managing Code Halos are not taught in any curriculum we know of, and they are not yet practiced with any consistency across companies worldwide. But this shift is the central challenge and opportunity for the next generation of business leaders. In the same manner that a senior executive must understand finance, sales, marketing, product development, operations, and strategy formulation, it is our view that generating value from the virtual, through Code Halos, should now be part of the managerial core curriculum. As our research highlights, it is the lever available to managers that currently generates—or destroys—more value than any other available.

The Code Halo opportunity is vast, and the downside for missing this trend will be harsh and swift. How you manage these dynamics during the next few years could define the arc of your career. Think ahead a decade, when people are sure to ask two questions: *Did you see this technology-based sea change coming? Were you able to capture the commercial opportunity?*

This book is intended to help you answer those questions:

Yes and *yes*.

PART I

DIGITS OVER WIDGETS: THE NEXT AGE OF BUSINESS AND TECHNOLOGY

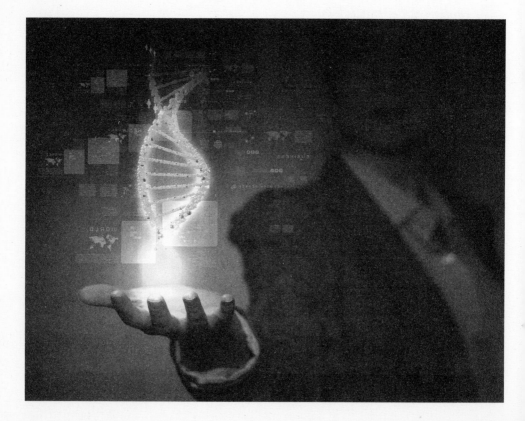

CHAPTER ONE

"Will It Happen to Us?" A Trillion-Dollar Opportunity or an Extinction Event

"Software is eating the world."

—Marc Andreessen[1]

Over the past decade, six technology-led companies have collectively generated more than $1 trillion of market value. Amazon, Apple, Facebook, Google, Netflix, and Pandora have leveraged consumer technologies in new ways—and in the process, have transformed customer expectations, established new operating models, and violently upended roughly a dozen mature industries. In the process, prior industry leaders—such as Nokia, Motorola, Borders, Barnes & Noble, AOL, Blockbuster, Tower Records, and HMV—lost, on average, more than 90% of their 2003 enterprise values. This value migration from one set of companies to another could not have been more forceful or final.

Most people have heard that part of the story. What they don't fully appreciate is the common denominator that sits at the heart of the business models of the Trillion-Dollar Club: the creation and management of Code Halos.

What Is a Code Halo?

A Code Halo is the field of digital information that surrounds any noun—any person, place, or thing. More often than not, that virtual self can provide more insight into—and thus generate more value from—the physical entity alone.

Take a simple but important example. There are tens of millions of people in the United States alone with some form of chronic respiratory condition who need to use inhalers every day. Mobile health platform Propeller Health has created a sensor that fits on these inhalers.[2] The system links to users' mobile devices to help track and manage their use of medication, and to send data to healthcare providers. The raw materials for each unit probably cost only a few dollars, but the value to users (and healthcare providers)—based on the data and information provided—could be literally priceless.

The members of the Trillion-Dollar Club have mastered the ability to create and manage the Code Halos surrounding their customers, products, services, and entire organizations to establish new thresholds of performance. In wrapping those widgets with digits, they have created highly personalized customer experiences, products, and services that deliver not just utility but also insight and meaning at unassailable levels of efficiency. It's how Pandora, without ever having met you, can play hours of your favorite music and how Netflix can recommend just the right film for your Sunday evening.

The First Trillion Is Always the Hardest

The first trillion dollars of market value these six companies have generated with this approach certainly won't be the last. Competing on the code that surrounds all products and people will continue to drive significant opportunity. W. Brian Arthur of the Santa Fe Institute and the Palo Alto Research Center (PARC) suggests that a vast, unseen digital economy is quickly emerging. This Second Economy—launched in 1995 with the commercialization of the Internet—will surpass the world's first (or industrial) economy in scale and scope by 2025.[3] That is, a virtual, digital economy will exceed the industrial economy—the cumulative output of mankind's development over several millennia— in terms of transactions, revenues, and value creation, in a mere *30 years*. It's clear that the Trillion-Dollar Club's accomplishments—over a relatively short space of time—are simply the beginning of this economic journey.

How Significant Was the Impact of the First Trillion Club?

The answer? *Very.* Consider the results of Apple, Amazon, Google, Facebook, Netflix, and Pandora, which in 2003 had a combined market capitalization of $34.3 billion. By 2013, this figure had exceeded $1.2 trillion. Apple's 2003 stock traded at $10 per share. By 2013, it was at least 40 times higher. Amazon went from $22 per share to $350. Netflix had just gone public with a sub-billion-dollar valuation in 2003; Google and Pandora were still venture-backed start-ups; and Facebook didn't even yet exist.

Ten years later, there had been a massive migration in value from one group of six companies to another (see Figure 1.1). And, of course, this simple analysis doesn't include other widget-based market leaders—such as Barnes & Noble, Motorola, Ericsson, Dell, and HMV—that suffered terribly in the face of Code Halo competitors.

The Trillion-Dollar Club

Code Halo Company	2003 Value (in Billions)[4]	2013 Value (in Billions)	Industrial Model Competitor	2003 Value (in Billions)	2013 Value (in Billions)
Amazon	$23.90	$180.20	Borders	$1.78	Bankrupt
Apple	$8.90	$515.40	Nokia	$87.50	$30.30
Facebook	Not yet founded	$132.00	MySpace[5]	$0.58	$0.04
Google	Private, four years old	$355.20	Yahoo!	$29.60	$37.50
Pandora	Private, three years old	$6.00	HMV[6]	$1.25	Bankrupt
Netflix	$1.5	$21.70	Blockbuster	$4.00	Bankrupt
Total	$34.30	$1,210.50	Total	$124.71	$67.84

Figure 1.1

Historical Sources of Competitive Advantage Don't Hold Up Well Against Code Halos

What is particularly noteworthy about this migration of value is that the Code Halo upstarts were competing against established leaders in their industries. We call these companies Widget Winners because their business models were based on traditional industrial approaches to making, distributing, selling, and managing physical goods and services. Once Code Halos took hold in their markets, a profound and unstoppable shift from widget-based business models to the digit-based Code Halo models took place.

In every case, the Widget Winners initially looked like they should have clobbered the digit-focused newcomers. The incumbents had all the advantages: brand awareness, established customer relationships, extensive distribution channels, research and development capabilities, management experience, employee depth, balance sheets, and market valuation.

In addition, what the Widget Winners and the new disrupters were selling was the same product in most cases. After all, Netflix and Blockbuster rented the same films; Amazon and Borders sold the same books; and the iPod and Microsoft's Zune were comparable machines. The Widget Winners held all the advantages, except the key one: they neglected to wrap their widgets with digits, to build digital business ecosystems, and to learn how to compete with Code Halos. As a result, the Widget Winners were vanquished by 2013—either bankrupt or mere shadows of their former selves. Blockbuster founder David Cook articulated this collapse well, lamenting that "It didn't have to be this way. They [Blockbuster] let technology eat them up."[7]

In hindsight, it wasn't even a fair fight. It was slaughter.

More Industries Heading to the Crossroads

All of these Widget Winner incumbents believed that their strategic and tactical positions meant that they were immune to the changes they could see happening all around them in the marketplace. They assumed the disruption others were suffering in the face of digitization wouldn't affect them. We often hear;

"It won't happen to us. Our industry is different."

No, it's not.

This value migration will not be contained to a handful of Silicon Valley *wunderkinds*. Although Code Halos first took hold in these highly technology-aware companies, they're becoming a universal platform for competition across most *all industries*.

For example: What provides you with more insight when choosing the right hospital for a particular surgery? Do you focus on the building's physical façade, its lobby, its marketing brochure, and what friends or family have told you about it? Or would you prefer to examine the rich halo of information—found on myriad online sources—providing objective and detailed views on its strongest practices, success rates on particular surgeries and physician quality? If you had a life-threatening condition, wouldn't you also want access to all of this information?

Code Halos Go Mainstream

The good news—for shareholders and employees—is that many traditional winners are already focusing on Code Halos. This is not because they are losing ground, but because they see this transition already happening and the scale of the opportunity ahead, as the Second Economy grows (see Figure 1.2). GE is not seriously threatened by an upstart builder of jet engines or power turbines, nor is Disney too worried about a venture-backed amusement park being built in Orlando. However, these firms recognize the power of Code Halos and the opportunity to insert these new capabilities into their existing business models to extend their market leadership.

Companies like these recognize that the Code Halo has become the key structural element of today's business models. It's what leads executives like GE CEO Jeff Immelt to comment, "Industrial companies, not just GE, but all industrial companies, are no longer just about the big iron.... All of us are going to seek to interface with the analytics, the data, [and] the software that surround our products."[8] And Mark Parker, the CEO of Nike, states, "The digital and physical worlds are starting to come together more seamlessly—it's only the tip of the iceberg in terms of what's coming."[9]

Code Halo Innovation in Established Leaders

Company	Industry and Initiative
GE	**Industrial goods** Through its "Industrial Internet" and "Brilliant Machines" initiatives, GE is creating Code Halos around industrial machines such as jet engines, locomotives, and power turbines.
Disney	**Hospitality** With its "MagicBands," Disney is creating a wearable wristband to generate Code Halos around its park guests, creating unique tailored experiences for these customers.
Allstate	**Insurance** Through its "Drivewise" in-car mobile telematics device, Allstate is building Code Halos around drivers and their cars, thus providing personalized auto insurance and rates.
Nike	**Fitness** With the Nike+ FuelBand—a wearable activity monitor—Nike is putting Code Halos around its customers, helping to analyze and improve their levels of personal fitness.

Figure 1.2

Code Halos: The Building Blocks of the Second Economy

Code Halos are becoming the key building blocks of the Second Economy. The industrial economy—from Watt's steam engine of 1775 through to Airbus's A380 of 2007—has been all about the design, manufacture, selling, and servicing of increasingly sophisticated physical products and services. The coming phase of commerce is now all about the virtual fields of information that surround people, products, places, and organizations. However, it is not only about building Code Halos around people and products. We must reimagine and reengineer the supporting organizational models and business processes to thrive in the new digital economy. In many cases, this transition will be a heavy lift, as established businesses will have to manage traditional ways along with the new. Yet ultimately, there is no choice for managing in these times of tremendous change.

Harnessing the Power of Code Halos in Your Industry

Would you rather have an iPhone or a BlackBerry? Work at Netflix or Blockbuster? Own stock in Facebook or Kodak? These questions seem silly. However, would you rather fly on United or Delta? Work at Aetna or The Hartford? Those are harder to answer. Yet in 10 years, the answers may be as easy as iPhone vs. BlackBerry. It will all boil down to which firms can master the new Second Economy and participate in their own Code Halo transformation, and which ones do not.

So the question is, "Will it happen to *us*?" We've seen what can happen if you do not embrace Code Halos: your organization can quickly find itself on the unrecoverable path to irrelevancy. On the other hand, if you do leverage these ideas and wrap your products, services, people, and devices with Code Halos, your organization will be well positioned for the extraordinary new commercial opportunities ahead.

As a first step in that journey, we'll take a closer look at our own personal Code Halos in Chapter 2.

CHAPTER TWO

The Personal Code Halo: Press "1" for the Real You

It's a strange and wonderful phenomenon: you're sitting at home, or perhaps at work, and you turn to your dazzling personal computing device. Within seconds, you're transported to a virtual yet incredibly real online world—one that's global, yet intimate. And although the device is driven by silicon and fiber, the experience feels remarkably human. Here you find friends, share ideas, conduct commerce, and delight in moments of genuine engagement.

As more of us spend more time online, we are increasingly integrating this highly personalized virtual world into our "real" world, often greatly enhancing the experience in both environments. As this happens, we're coming to recognize that the technologies making such an engagement possible—broadband networks, mobility, and social computing—are transforming our lives by allowing us to blend the virtual and real worlds. They alter and enhance how we connect with friends, ask for directions, collaborate with colleagues, consume media—even exercise. Personal technology has enhanced so many aspects of our personal lives.

But not how we get our cash.

You make your way to your local bank branch where you've been a customer for 15 years and, upon inserting your bank card in the ATM, the first thing you see is *Press 1 for English. Press 2 for Spanish.*

Really? This sophisticated financial services institution, with billions in assets and branches around the world, this behemoth that claims it is your *partner,* doesn't know what language you speak? It knows your checking and savings account balances. It tracks your spending habits well enough to cut off your debit card when it notices something out of the ordinary. It holds a loan on your car and your home, knows how much you're worth, and has records of every transaction you've made since 1998—but it doesn't know what language you speak.

It may seem like a minor inconvenience, but this exchange shows that most bank ATMs, and even bank tellers, only know what's in their systems of record, rather than what is in your Code Halo. They may know your transactional data in isolation, but it certainly feels as if they don't *know you* and your real financial life.

Visiting the bank can leave you with an incredibly disconnected feeling. What happened to that pleasing online world you were visiting just a few moments ago? And why is it that younger, technology-led companies like Pandora, Amazon, Hulu, and Netflix that understand that world know all about us? Not only what language we speak, but our likes and dislikes and much of our personal profile in ways that were unimaginable just a few years ago.

They know these things because they can see something an ATM, or even a bank teller, can't. They see our Code Halos.

Invisible But Always Present, Ever Enriching

Everyone has a Code Halo. How is it formed? What does it contain?

Think first of the many computing devices you use in your everyday life—your tablet, smartphone, console, laptop. Now consider all the things you do with them: connect with friends and colleagues, manage your to-do lists, read books and explore content, play games, work, watch movies and videos, listen to music, monitor your fitness, get directions, buy products.

Now picture the digital information that constantly flows between all your devices. Every click, swipe, tap, and keystroke you make gathers information around you and your gadgets. Over time, highly individualized patterns and detailed correlations emerge. This unique accumulation and configuration of data becomes your virtual identity: your personal Code Halo.

Many individuals and companies recognize and cultivate their own Code Halos by sharing information actively, while others are still largely unaware of them. Some companies also have the ability to see yours. Other more traditional companies, like the bank with the language-challenged ATM, are blind to Code Halos and continue to treat their customers and partners with arm's-length anonymity.

Take Us, for Example

This all may sound a little mystical, so let's discuss something tangible. When one of the three of us walks into a store, this is what the salespeople see:

Store associates might make general inferences like: "Here is a middle-aged, white male who's dressed somewhat conservatively." That's about it. An especially experienced, ambitious, or well-trained salesperson might engage in the black art of selling by asking some "qualifying" questions or by applying their knowledge of psychographics to our body language, how we speak, or the style of our clothing. But no matter how much these salespeople are able to divine from such physical clues, their interactions with us will likely be driven by erroneous assumptions based on extremely limited data. This purely physical interpretation of a customer is highly limiting—and judging us solely based on our appearance will likely result in uniform, nonpersonalized treatment. After all, by the primary demographic slices, we appear to be pretty much the same.

But here is what Amazon, Netflix, Apple, Pandora, Facebook, or Google sees each time they "look" at us:

Individual Code Halos yield a rich picture that transcends a simple physical impression.

Individual Code Halos yield a rich picture that transcends a simple physical impression. Organizations that see customers in this manner can create highly personalized interactions by analyzing our past buying behaviors, the songs we like, our searches, histories, media preferences, and even our geographic location. For instance, although this book's three authors *appear* to be quite similar, we actually have quite divergent tastes and interests. Paul likes jazz and cycling. Malcolm is bored by jazz and wishes his neighborhood wasn't clogged with MAMILs on a Sunday morning (middle aged men in Lycra, if you were wondering). Ben enjoys reading novels such as Will Self's *Umbrella*, which just seems too much like hard work to Paul and Malcolm. It's clear that selling to all three of us in the same manner would bore, irritate, or even offend us. But linking elements of our Code Halos allows brands to improve a specific shopping experience.

When firms such as Amazon and Google interact with our rich virtual selves, they recognize these striking differences between the three of us. They understand particular tastes, likes, and dislikes in many areas of life that provide distinct gradations and insight into our true needs. As such, they can deliver custom, curated experiences. They create those "Aha!" moments of insight, in which it feels they are ahead of us or even, at times, inside our heads.

It's strange that for many, the in-person has become so impersonal, and the virtual so intimate. Yet that is the power of Code Halos.

This is why walking the aisles of Sears or Macy's feels so utterly inefficient and impersonal after shopping at Amazon. It's why waiting to talk to someone at a call center—and having to enter your account number multiple times—feels antiquated and ridiculous. It's why having to renew a passport, file a tax return, make an insurance claim, do your expenses, or fill out your kids' new school-year paperwork feels like you're stepping back into your parents' world. It's strange that for many, the in-person has become so impersonal, and the virtual so intimate. Yet that is the power of Code Halos.

When Code Meets Code …

So how *do* brands create these moments of precise insight? How can Pandora design such accurate and personalized radio stations when they only know a few of your favorite songs? How does Amazon recommend a list of your favorite films, even when you've never rented a film from its site? How can these companies make correlations that lead to insights about needs, behaviors, wants, or potentialities that were not obvious before?

Such personal insights are generated by Code Halo connections, the intersection of the rich information in one form of Code Halo—the consumer—with that of another like a company. For example, when you interact with iTunes, the information you've shared about your tastes in music, literature, and movies, combined with your geographic location, demographics, reading interests, social network connections, and information about the devices you use, presents iTunes with a rich Code Halo that defines who you are well beyond your music preferences.

If that were the end of the interaction, it would not be a fusion; it would be an "information capture" by the company. But iTunes has its own Code Halo, a massive field of information containing millions of customers' musical likes and transactions, extensive knowledge accumulated through its Big Data initiatives, and insights gained by its sophisticated proprietary algorithms. Through such engines, it sees patterns in the many correlations embedded within its customer data. In our example above, if Malcolm shows a liking for grunge music, iTunes will then realize his taste in movies aligns very closely with the Academy Award nominees. Similarly, once Paul starts downloading a lot of Jimi Hendrix, it knows there's a good chance he will like its sci-fi movie recommendations.

When the two codes connect, iTunes recognizes the patterns in your Code Halo and instantly creates the tailored user experience you have now come to expect—one that's so different from the frustrating encounter with the neighborhood bank.

The SMAC Stack: Driver of the Technological Sea Change

These highly personalized digital experiences that can only happen when code connects with code have emerged in recent years because they are built on four technologies that have only lately become mainstream: social, mobile, analytics, and cloud—or SMAC—that work together as an integrated technology stack. Information created, managed, and shared via these technologies is pouring into the enterprise at a velocity that is causing whiplash even for many market-leading companies with technology mastery at their core.

We'll go into more detail on the SMAC Stack in Chapter 5, but a few facts paint the picture of how large and pervasive this technology architecture is becoming (see Figure 2.1).

Growth of the SMAC Stack

The SMAC Stack	Market Impact
Social	– Facebook had 1.15 billion active users as of July 2013, 699 million of whom use the service daily.[1] – Two companies, Netflix and YouTube, account for half of the daily Internet traffic in the United States.[2]
Mobile	– There will be approximately 8 billion mobile devices in use by 2016, and by 2020, there will be some 50 billion interconnected devices.[3] – Apple's iPhones and Google Android devices had sold a combined 1.473 billion units through August 2013.[4]
Analytics	– Ninety percent of the world's information has been generated in the past two years, and 80 percent of it is unstructured.[5] – We create 2.5 exabytes of data each day.[6] To put this in perspective, one exabyte equals 50,000 years' worth of DVD-quality video.[7] – Between 2009 and 2020, the amount of data being managed will grow at least 50-fold.[8]
Cloud	– In the month of July 2013, Pandora's customers listened to nearly 1.3 billion hours of music.[9] – By 2016, two-thirds of all global data center traffic will be cloud-based.[10]

Figure 2.1

In short, SMAC technologies are the infrastructure of the new Code Halo economy. And similar to the interstate highway system built in the 1950s and 1960s, this new foundation is being built very quickly.

However, creating Code Halos requires more than just deploying this stack of technologies. Mobile devices without social networks cannot create connections; data that doesn't make sense is just noise. Analytics without business intent creates little more than static. For a Code Halo to have an impact on performance, it must be integrated into well-codified and well-understood business processes—such as sales, customer service, research and development, or supply-chain management.

The Discipline of Creating Value from Insight

Yet Code Halos' value proposition goes far beyond enabling certain processes to run better, faster, and cheaper. The most important ingredient that allowed Code Halo masters to win their markets and build so much value? *They created highly individualized experiences by managing on the meaning of the Code Halo.*

But what is "managing on meaning?" In a pedestrian sense, "making meaning" in business is the development of personalized goods and services. We accomplish this not only by industrial rules—delivering the best product or services possible at attractive price points to certain demographics—but now by Code Halo rules: recognizing and fully understanding customers' very personal needs and determining how to connect with those needs one customer at a time.

We can find meaning-making potential almost everywhere; the information surrounding every individual, product, and organization is fantastically rich with clues and cues about past behavior, current needs, and future possibilities.

Products without meaning are simply a reflection of their makers. For example, a basic kitchen blender is the same blender, whether it's sold in America, Belgium, or Chile. All it reflects is its own manufacturer—the design aesthetics, manufacturing capabilities, and value-for-money of that company. On the other hand, **products with meaning are not just reflections of their makers, but also become reflections of their consumers.** In time, one person's Facebook page becomes wildly different from another's. A smartphone becomes a very personal device, and Amazon recommendations become highly individualized. You begin to hear this personalization in the way people talk: "*My* phone, *my* Facebook page, *my* Twitter feed."

By infusing their products and services with individual meaning, the members of the Trillion-Dollar Club have rendered dumb products smart, turned interactions into experiences, and generated insights from information that previously seemed pedestrian or random. In doing so, their products and services reflect each customer's individuality, becoming an extension of that person's needs, networks, and beliefs.

We can find meaning-making potential almost everywhere; the information surrounding every individual, product, and organization is fantastically rich with clues and cues about past behavior, current needs, and future possibilities. But we must actively cultivate meaning through analysis and interpretation. This allows organizations to create value based on insight.

"Managing meaning" was at the heart of the market flip in mobile phones between Widget Winners (Nokia, Motorola, and Ericsson) and Code Halo Winners (Apple and Samsung). Despite the rise of the smartphone after 2005, Nokia and the others continued to go to market in an industrial manner—in trading on hardware, on the features, performance, and price of their phones. Their phones were all about *them*.

Apple, on the other hand, made meaning for its customers through virtual experiences based on software. The company's hardware—the industrial manifestation of its efforts—was simply the means to the end of creating meaningful and individualized customer experiences through software. The Apple phone was all about its owner; it served as a window into one's virtual world. In leveraging software to integrate your music, photos, social networks, and phone onto one platform, the iPhone enhanced users' physical lives by helping build their digital lives. Indeed, it was *physically* beautiful; but it also created a beautiful customer experience over time. In short, Apple was competing on the value of the virtual while Nokia was still competing on widgets. And we all know how that story ended.

Code Halos: A New Core Competency

Code Halos have initially emerged in our personal lives but are now beginning to impact large companies, start-ups, schools, governments, and mid-sized businesses. It is imperative that all organizations learn this new game. As we already recognize through our personal experiences, our Code Halos will have us interacting with people and institutions that:

- Know who we are as well as our preferences, characteristics, and associations.
- Understand how we like to interact and how we don't.
- Direct us effortlessly to what we are looking for.
- Anticipate and extrapolate about what we *might* be looking for or interested in.
- Remember every detail of our interaction, including the high points and low points, in order to improve the next one.
- Create an experience that is genuinely helpful to us rather than self-serving to the company.

"Decoding" your customers' Code Halos— understanding in fine-grain detail who they are and what they value—is becoming the new way to win in business.

Personal Code Halos Showcase Value of the Virtual

Code Halos around us as individuals are familiar, valuable, and fun. They are also sources of tremendous value for the pioneers of the Trillion-Dollar Club. Today's winning businesses are figuring out that it's no longer enough to compete on a great product and great people alone. They recognize that the information that your customers create and share with you, that your products and services generate, and that your company is producing generate unprecedented new levels of insight and business meaning when properly harnessed. "Decoding" your customers' Code Halos—understanding in fine-grain detail who they are and what they value—is becoming the new way to win in business.

This story started in our personal lives, but the next phase of innovation is happening in organizations that are creating advantage by applying Code Halo thinking to a broader array of "things" and business processes. To imagine that Code Halos can only be applied to relatively simple activities such as book or music retailing would be a fundamental, strategic, error. The Code Halo story is much more important than that. In the next chapter, we'll explore the five Code Halos that are reshaping the organization as we know it.

CHAPTER THREE

The Five Business Code Halos: Connecting Customers, Products, and Organizations

Code Halos are as much about products, services, employees, and entire organizations as they are about customers. We see five types of Code Halo solutions emerging.

- **Customer** Code Halos: the new basis of customer relationships.
- **Product** Code Halos: shifting value from widgets to digits.
- **Employee** Code Halos: allowing team members to connect and solve problems in new ways.
- **Partner** Code Halos: enabling ecosystem members to connect and form value webs for new levels of innovation and efficiency.
- **Enterprise** Code Halos: the new brand aggregators.

This chapter will review each of these five Code Halos in depth. You'll likely recognize immediate applicability of at least one or two of them to your organization.

The Customer Code Halo: The Relationship Maker

We know that our personal Code Halos create a digital key that, when applied to the right lock, can open up incredible new experiences and enhanced value. An enterprise's customer Code Halo—such as the profile a company has about you and other customers similar to you— is that lock.

Companies are able to capture and leverage consumer data to generate personalized customer experiences by using sophisticated algorithms that they apply to individualized code. For example,

Amazon's "Betterizer" system pioneered the customer Code Halo and led the way in designing the Amazon experience around the customer, rather than around the company.

Amazon's Betterizer is simple, transparent, and easy to use. Here's what you find at Amazon.com:[1]

amazon.com

Take a minute to improve your shopping experience by telling us which things you like. This helps us provide you with more personalized product recommendations.

Things you like on Amazon are private and won't be shared without your permission.

How to use it:

Click the "Like" button below any item that interests you. We'll note it and replace it with another item we hope you'll also like.

If you see an item you're not interested in, hover on it, and then select "Not interested." We'll show you something else instead.

Click "Refresh and show different items" to see a new selection of items.

To see your personalized product recommendations, click "Show my new recommendations."

Want to tell us about a specific item to help improve your recommendations? Here's How

Source: © Amazon.com

By engaging with Amazon, a customer elects to gain a more personalized and curated shopping experience. Amazon, in turn, not only builds a stronger relationship with the individual customer; it also makes its institutional Code Halo more robust and accurate. As a result, Amazon states it is able to ensure an excellent shopping experience by presenting you "with the right items in the right place at the right time." You'll want to remember this phrase: providing the **right information at the right place at the right time** is a central tenet in all forms of Code Halo implementations.

Companies large and small that focus on the digital experience are following the path Amazon blazed by constructing algorithms around the now-familiar phrases "You might also like" and "Customers who bought X also bought Y." Such constructs are now flooding into companies that hardly count as "born-digital."

Disney, for example, is launching a MagicBand bracelet to help guide visitors through its amusement parks, manage ticketing, personalize the guest experience, and even work as a portable bank. The MagicBand is set to transform a day at a Disney park from a one-size-fits-all experience into a highly personalized one. This new feature is at the center of Disney's new "vacation management" system called MyMagic+, which consists of a My Disney Experience website, an app, and the bracelet. Guests can visit the website to plan every aspect of their Disney vacation in advance by entering preferences, likes, and personal information. Once at the park, visitors use the smartphone app to adjust plans and make the most out of their visit. The MagicBand is your key to the kingdom: it will get you into the park as well as your hotel room, learn your favorite rides and characters, and serve as your way to pay for dining and shopping.

As the number of interconnected things expands, almost every device, product, and object—from simple consumer goods to complex industrial equipment—is a candidate for a Code Halo.

MyMagic+ also provides a complete story of the guest's interaction for Disney. Every bit of information about a particular visitor is contained in one place and is far richer and more comprehensive than credit card info that tracks transactions, or phone data that tracks general locations. My Magic+ allows Disney to track every ride you take, the staff interactions you have, each meal you eat and item you purchase, and the times you go back to your room to relax. As guests feed data into Disney, the company builds a rich database of wants and desires, allowing it to create ever-more-enjoyable experiences for its guests through better data profiling, more granular segmentation, and targeted commercial interactions.

Product Code Halos Shift Value from Widgets to Digits

The concept of the Code Halos that surround people—whether they are leading their personal, noncommercial lives or acting as consumers—is relatively easy to grasp. However, Code Halos also bring the "Internet of Things" (IoT) to life, and by 2020 we will have more Code Halos around products than customers.[2] As the number of interconnected things expands, almost every device, product, and object—from simple consumer goods to complex industrial equipment—is a candidate for a Code Halo.

There's already a huge number of connected devices. Today there are more than 10 billion things connected to the Internet; by 2020, that number will grow to 50 billion.[3] This vast IP-enabled product infrastructure allows us to now add intelligence to almost any object or device and connect it to the Internet.

The list of potential IoT examples grows by the day—and their application is seemingly limitless. When it comes to your company's product portfolio, almost everything is up for grabs. Code Halos connect the IoT so that value, insight, and meaning can emerge over time. These products—"software" in many cases—will become more valuable than their associated "hardware." Consider a smart toothbrush. The physical tool itself is a commodity, but a user's brushing habits, dental hygiene history, and health needs create a halo of information of premium value.

It's now easy and affordable to wrap products with Code Halos. The question for all of us will soon become not, "What should I wrap with a Code Halo?" but rather, "What should I NOT wrap with a Code Halo?"

The example of the Nest thermostat exemplifies how a standard product is transformed once it is instrumented, connected to the Internet, and surrounded by its own Code Halo. Dubbed the "learning thermostat," Nest is a home heating management system for the iPod generation; in fact, the brain behind Nest, Tony Fadell, designed the iPod.[4] Once installed—which customers can easily do themselves—the Nest Learning Thermostat keeps track of every adjustment you make to the temperature. After a week or so, Nest begins to understand your household's routines and rhythms. It learns when you get up in the morning and whether you like the bathroom warm or bracing. It records when you leave home and how low you want the temperature to remain while you're away. It discovers when you typically return home, what temperature you prefer at dinnertime, and takes note of your bedtimes and your preferred sleeping temperature. You tell it what kind of heating system you have—forced hot air, radiant, heat pump, or dual fuel—and Nest helps you get the most from it by reminding you when to change your filters, for example. Users can remotely control Nest via their computing device. Nest emails usage reports and statistics to you, and advises on ways you can better manage your heating and cooling costs. The device claims to cut energy costs by about 15% for the typical family—precisely because it knows there is no typical family. As validation of the growing role and value of Code Halos around connected devices, Google purchased the four-year-old company for $3.2 billion in early 2014.

What Nest has done with the thermostat can be accomplished with almost any product. Importantly, this approach introduces a new chapter of opportunity for manufacturers of all kinds of products or devices. Cars are evolving into mobile computing platforms. Aircraft engines are communicating about their performance. Athletic clothing is monitoring your pulse and guiding your golf swing.[5] Your body is— or will soon be—sending you messages to help you ensure that you're taking the right medicine for your heart condition, thereby keeping you out of the hospital.[6]

The IoT, however, is not really just *about* things. Rather, it's about the **value** we get in our personal lives—staying healthy, managing our finances, connecting with friends—as well as the business value that's unlocked when the devices connect to other things or to people. From mobile phones to aircraft engines, and even to personal grooming tools such as toothbrushes, more and more of today's devices are becoming network-aware.[7] And all have the potential to generate rich Code Halos that interact with the halos of information from people, business processes, and organizations—thereby producing streams of data that are ripe for deriving meaning.

Employee Code Halos: New Ways for Team Members to Connect and Solve Problems

As we've seen, personal Code Halos enrich our consumer experience; similarly, employee Code Halos have the potential to enrich our work experience. The employee Code Halo can contain your work history, subject matter expertise, affiliations and associations, projects and programs, perspectives, writings and presentations, work styles, and experiences. We can then use these halos to generate effective and flexible models for conducting knowledge work. They facilitate getting the right work (properly contextualized) to the right person at the right time, and assuring that the individual doing the work is armed with the proper organizational assets available to do his or her job most effectively. In much the same way that Amazon's consumer Code Halos and algorithms individualize the shopping experience, employee halos and organizational algorithms will individualize and transform—even revolutionize—the work experience.

Google is pioneering the development of employee Code Halos specifically to improve human resource processes. Despite Google's much-vaunted employee management methods, the company recognizes that the hiring, firing, and retiring methods in most organizations (including large ones) are, to say the least, unscientific. After all, we still hear axioms such as "You're hired for your résumé, but fired for your personality." Google's goal is to apply its data-driven perspective to engineering challenges to its people management.[8] That means encouraging employees to share such information as work and personal preferences, likes, transactions, and comments, just as they would with entertainment providers or banks or airlines. Google expects that the insights it gains from analyzing this information will enable it to create the corporate employee equivalent of meaningful customer experiences: sharper articulation of career expectations and preferences, more appropriately customized benefits packages, better matches between individuals and working units or projects, and a better understanding of distress and success factors.

Another important example of the employee Code Halo is the role that professional networking site LinkedIn plays in making information about career history, achievement, and trajectory more open and transparent. Your LinkedIn profile has become the de facto résumé and dossier; it's the primary and most effective way of informing a huge network of colleagues, partners, clients, and employers who you are, what you do, where you've been, and where you're going, or would like to go. As the reliance on LinkedIn increases, the printers of business cards lament.

After a long period of slow but unspectacular growth, LinkedIn has exploded in usage in the past two years as it has added deeper, broader, and richer functionality into its offering. The site has positioned itself as a central platform of employee-to-employee and employee-to-employer communication. Whether LinkedIn is able to maintain and extend its platform remains to be seen. What is certain, however, is that the company's Code Halo approach has sparked the entire HR industry into thinking about fresh, improved ways of maximizing value from the most valuable of resources (even in a Code Halo world): people. This is much more than merely "Facebook at work." Creating and managing employee Code Halos will help dramatically improve productivity, retention, and hiring.

The Partner Code Halo: Weaver of Webs

To both innovate rapidly and lower costs, companies in life sciences, banking, insurance, healthcare, and manufacturing are using cutting-edge technologies to create more efficient and effective partner ecosystems. With new technologies (including the SMAC Stack) and more collaborative mind-sets, traditional supply chains—primarily linear and designed for physical products—are re-forming into tightly integrated systems for sharing and co-creating knowledge assets. Leaders in many industries have succeeded by rethinking their production processes to exploit virtualized ways of working.

The twenty-first-century "social enterprise" is becoming a virtual business that favors specialist partners over in-house teams, production capabilities distributed globally, and just-in-time logistics for production and fulfillment over stockpiling and large inventories. The concept of partner Code Halos is a natural platform to enable this transition.

We can think of the partner Code Halo as a metaset of product and employee Code Halos. Individual objects and devices—from microcomponents to whole manufacturing lines—can generate information through RFID (Radio Frequency Identification) about their location and condition. Social networks can be created around specific components and products, enabling engineers all along the supply chain to collaborate better. The synchronization of delivery times, which is crucial to just-in-time environments, is enhanced as Code Halo intersections across every segment of a supply chain—from shipping data to traffic conditions—bring greater clarity and insight to real-time decision-making.

The Enterprise Code Halo: Brand Aggregator

The final Code Halo is the enterprise Code Halo itself. In a way, this is an aggregate of the four others—customer, product, employee, and partner—that paints a dynamic and accurate picture of what the enterprise does and how it does it. Your organization's identity is increasingly defined by information in your enterprise Code Halo.

Angry customer comments, complimentary media coverage, financial results, and data from thousands of other sources create a perception of your company that is as real as the bricks and rebar of your manufacturing plant.

Every day, information about your products, clients, partners, and employees creates or destroys value. Angry customer comments, complimentary media coverage, financial results, and data from thousands of other sources create a perception of your company that is as real as the bricks and rebar of your manufacturing plant. In many ways, the enterprise Code Halo is stronger, clearer, and more compelling than the efforts of your traditional marketing department.

In the Code Halo economy, transparency reaches a level at which companies can simply no longer employ old—and sometimes misleading—marketing tricks. For example, a terrible movie that could once find an audience through *contextomy* (the selective excerpting of words from their original context that distorts the source's intended meaning) can't get away with that anymore.

One such film, *Norbit* (starring Eddie Murphy), released in 2007, was promoted with the blurb "Eddie Murphy's comic skills are immense" splashed across the movie poster. What the poster omitted was that the review this quote was taken from—by the *Chicago Tribune*'s Michael Wilmington—actually said, "Eddie Murphy's comic skills are immense ... So why does he want to make these huge, belching spectaculars, movies as swollen, monstrous and full of hot air as Rasputia (his character in the movie) herself—here misdirected by Brian Robbins ...?"[9] Today, the Code Halo of a movie would expose such a blatant lie immediately through friends' comments on social sites, review aggregation sites such as Rotten Tomatoes, and near-real-time box office data. Businesses now face the reality that their Code Halos say more about them than a trophy-building new ad campaign, or a snazzy annual report ever could—for good or ill.

Many organizations have historically worked hard to stay out of the public spotlight. Whether high-priced management consultants, hedge funds, or political operatives, these types of operations will face challenges adjusting to a world in which openness reigns. Chapter 9 will discuss in detail the way in which these entities will find it difficult to adjust to a world where customers regard secrecy with suspicion, and favor—in fact, *expect*—openness and transparency as positive cultural norms.

The Hype and the Reality of *Norbit*

Tomatometer	All Critics	Audience
9%	Coming off his Oscar-nominated performance in Dreamgirls, the talented but inconsistent Eddie Murphy, plays three roles in Norbit, a cruel, crass, stereotype-filled comedy that's more depressing than funny.	**54%**
Average Rating: **3.3**/10 Reviews Counted: **126** Fresh: **11** | Rotten: **112**		**Liked it** Average Rating: **3**/5 User Rating: **657,284**

Source: © Rottentomatoes.com, Inc. All rights reserved.

The enterprise Code Halo will be the dominant source of market truth for today's organizations. Marketing will become less about writing ad copy and more about managing the corporate Code Halo. While this may be a stomach-churning thought for many current senior leaders, denying this truth is no defense—and customers will dismiss attempts to spin the facts as the work of "the designated corporate liars." It will be—indeed, already is—necessary to face the reality that customers, partners, employees, and regulators will be a central factor in determining how value propositions are generated and how companies communicate with the market. Leaders who are able to manage the enterprise Code Halo and who know how to balance "gives" and "gets" will likely find themselves in positions of power and influence. Those who ignore the Code Halo may find themselves at their own personal crossroads.

Five Halos Matter to People, Places, and Things

Code Halos may have emerged from our personal lives and use of consumer technologies, but they are rapidly changing how organizations connect to customers and each other to generate value. Although the diverse range of Code Halos may look very different—indeed are very different—on closer examination, each one has the same five essential characteristics. We'll look at these characteristics in the next chapter.

CHAPTER FOUR

The Anatomy of a Winning Code Halo Solution

It's tempting to look at a product or service that you have in place or are developing and declare it a Code Halo solution if it contains one or more SMAC Stack elements such as mobility or analytics or an element of social media technology. But the presence of some of the parts of the stack does not constitute a total Code Halo solution. The five essential elements that form the anatomy of a Code Halo *solution* are outlined in Figure 4.1—and they must work in harmony to thrive and deliver the desired result.

Five Elements of a Code Halo Solution

Halo Element	Role
Amplifier	Any device that can capture, generate, and manage Code Halo information.
Application Interface	How the device, solution, and user intersect—crucial to the user experience.
Algorithm	This decodes the rivers of data that flow through a Code Halo.
Data	The raw material of analysis and meaning-making.
Business Model	This defines how companies "monetize meaning."

Figure 4.1

Individual implementations balance these elements in different ways. Some Code Halo solutions, like Google for example, may have massive amounts of data and highly complex algorithms, with standard amplifiers and simple application interfaces. Others require customized and sophisticated amplifiers and application interfaces, yet thrive on simple algorithms, like Nike+ FuelBand. Whatever the solution, all the elements need to be there, working together.

The Amplifier: The Internet of Things Is a Network of Code Halo Amplifiers

The starting point for a successful Code Halo solution is the Amplifier: the physical device or object that serves as a platform to capture and transmit data. We think of these devices—the "things"—as amplifiers because they help manage, create, intensify, and share Code Halos. As the Internet of Things (IoT) grows, devices beyond just "computers" are becoming the hardware platform for Code Halos.

Code Halos require simple, beautiful, amplifier devices. They need to be easy to set up and use to allow for quick market adoption and viral growth; they must be intuitive, elegant, and able to fit easily into the rhythm of the user's personal or business life. If the amplifier is clumsy, slows people down, or forces them to spend more than 10 minutes learning how to use it, you've lost before you've started.

The key to an effective amplifier is that it is a "daily use" device. It must be something that customers, employees, or machines will use in their ordinary activities—such as getting directions, preparing for a sales call, or making a delivery in a truck.

To date, most amplifiers have been computing devices and thus gave rise to consumer-based eBusiness Code Halos for companies in the Trillion-Dollar Club. In hindsight, this made perfect sense; these firms were able to leverage a preexisting infrastructure of amplifiers. There was no need to ask customers to purchase or Internet-enable a new device, since they already possessed and were using them. In the future, the types of amplifier will become more diverse, but there will be four main types:

- **Computing devices:** Computers, tablets, and smartphones are established Code Halo amplifiers.
- **Wearables** like Google Glass, The Nike+ FuelBand, Disney's MagicBand, and smart watches from Samsung and Apple.
- **Industrial machines** that have been IP-enabled, such as factory equipment, locomotives, and jet engines.
- **Consumer machines** such as dishwashers, cars, and thermostats.

Computing Devices Are Today's Established Amplifiers

We have all participated in the computing device growth story. There has been an explosion of desktops and laptops since the early 1990s. Then came the dramatic surge in popularity of the tablet,[1] which fundamentally altered the device landscape.

It's not only the device landscape that's changing rapidly; the **user scene** is also in transition. Before 2000, a major percentage of laptop and desktop use was associated with corporations. But as processing power increased and costs fell, computer use spread to the general population. Nowadays, more than 2.4 billion people stay connected by using desktops, laptops, and mobile devices.[2] About 70% of U.S. homes have broadband connectivity.[3]

Anatomy Lesson #1: If it costs more than $50, and you can't eat it, put a Code Halo around it.

Moore's Law—which states that over the history of computing hardware, the number of transistors on integrated circuits doubles approximately every two years[4]—has come to the IoT. The cost of Bluetooth or IP-enabling most any product is negligible and steadily dropping. Our recommendation is that any product that costs more than $50 should have the ability to communicate on a continual basis with the Internet. Think about daily use devices that are already instrumented: watches, toothbrushes, toys, dog collars, and soccer balls. This list will go on and on over the coming years.

The "Skinterface" Will Change the Consumer Experience

Most of us wear "dumb" devices every day: watches, glasses, belts, shoes, coats. Each of those items is about to get very smart.

Google Glass, for example, allows you to "see" much more than what lies physically before you. This device will help answer the questions that constantly pop into our minds as we go about our daily lives: *What kind of tree is that in the park? What companies occupy that building? What is the story of the artist who created this sculpture?*

Your body becomes the next technology miracle; think of it as your "skinterface." Your watch will double as a health monitor. Your shirt will sense your body temperature and adjust the heating in your living room to a comfortable level.[5] A sports bra currently on the market uses sensor technology for early detection of breast cancer.[6]

The widespread adoption of wearable amplifiers will likely have an effect on adjacent market sectors, just as computing devices—particularly smartphones—have had a devastating effect on the low-end camera, GPS, and wristwatch markets.

Industrial Amplifiers: Harnessing the Power of the Internet of Things

In much the same way that wearables can enhance consumers' lives, IP-enabling can greatly enhance the "lives" of complex industrial machines. GE calls its versions Brilliant Machines and sees huge potential in their commercial value.

> GE estimates that the Industrial Internet could add up to $15 trillion to global GDP in productivity gains over the next 15 years. Norfolk Southern, for example, is using a GE data and analytics system to optimize train and cargo movement across its rail network. The railroad says every 1 mph increase in network speed could save $200 million in annual capital and operating expenses.[7]

These estimates seem conservative. When an industrial machine—whether it's a locomotive, jet engine, tractor trailer, road grader, steel stamper, or power turbine—gets smart, it performs better, with greater uptime, longevity, and utilization. This can have a profound impact on the bottom line of the manufacturers of these machines—and, more importantly, those who use them.

Smart Appliances Become Amplifiers in the Home

My $300 phone is so smart, but my $30,000 car is so dumb. You may have thought this. We certainly have. However, we won't think this at all by 2018. Your refrigerator, for example, will become a food management system. It will alert you when the lettuce is wilting or when you should put the meat in the freezer, remind you that the milk is running out, suggest meals you can cook from what you have on hand, and keep track of how you're doing on the weekly grocery budget. It will help you monitor and manage your health by tracking your consumption of healthy foods versus your consumption of ice cream and beer.

Almost every machine in your life will soon become a smart machine.

Other "smart" machines will offer ways to save users money. For instance, good drivers often wonder why they should have to pay to insure poor drivers. After all, if you adhere to the law and have a safe driving record, your current insurance policy means that you're simply underwriting those who fail to do so. Progressive Insurance's Snapshot initiative and Allstate's Drivewise program have introduced telematics devices—Code Halo amplifiers in the auto insurance space—that allow good drivers to derive the benefits of their safe driving.[8]

Your car, major home appliances, HVAC system, lawnmower, swimming pool—the examples abound. The bottom line: Almost every machine in your life will soon become a smart machine.

The Application Interface: Window to a Beautiful Experience

While the amplifier creates and manages information, the **application interface** draws users toward a Code Halo solution.

For example, the Nike+ FuelBand you can wear on your wrist is the amplifier that, through its embedded motion sensors, records your daily movements. However, the FuelBand itself provides only basic information. It is the FuelBand's application interface—which lives on a computing device—that makes detailed analysis and personal insights possible. Netflix customers receive movie recommendations via an application on their mobile devices, TVs, tablets, and laptops. American Airlines maintenance engineers check the status of engine repairs, and homeowners with the Nest thermostat track their energy cost savings, through beautiful application interfaces.

We call these application interfaces because they are what users—customers, partners, employees—actually *touch* at a moment of engagement. And it is through this interface that the Code Halo—and the value it delivers—is displayed. Early Code Halo solutions consisted of a basic amplifier (a laptop or desktop), and the interface was generally a Web browser. The two components were integrated but limited in what they could do, since they were primarily platforms for eCommerce transactions with some associated analytics activities. Now, firms creating Code Halo solutions manage the amplifiers and application interfaces elements distinctly.

We'll go into more depth on the importance of creating a beautiful experience—including the application through which people engage with Code Halos—in Chapter 8; but this element of the complete experience is critical to the success of a Code Halo solution.

Yet how do brands derive such intelligence from oceans of data? Through the **algorithm.**

The Algorithm: Data Becomes Meaning

Data without an algorithm is like hieroglyphics without a Rosetta Stone.

The **algorithm**—a set of logic equations and analysis processes designed to answer specific business questions—is a Code Halo's brain. Like the Rosetta Stone, which enabled scholars to decode the ancient language of hieroglyphs, the algorithm allows decision-makers to separate the signal—**what matters**—from the noise. Yet algorithms go beyond simple decoding (such as statistical analyses of historical information across key market segments or product sets) by helping us recognize previously unseen patterns. Code Halo algorithms start to provide *predictive* views on individuals. And that's what establishes those "they read my mind" moments of magic.

Anatomy Lesson #2: Algorithms are the foundation of the Code Halo experience.

The algorithm may be the most important of the five elements of a Code Halo anatomy, as it provides lasting uniqueness and competitive advantage. Amplifiers are relatively easy to copy; interfaces start to look similar over time. And if your competitors are any good, they'll accumulate lots of Big Data. However, the right algorithms become a reflection of your management talent and insight—what do you measure, how do you measure it, and what do you then do with your conclusions? As such, competitive advantage with amplifiers, interfaces, and data might seem potentially short-lived; but if done right, distinctions based on algorithms can be lasting.

The algorithm is the "secret sauce" of a successful Code Halo solution. A properly constructed algorithm recognizes patterns in massive sets of data, determines cause and effect, and creates meaning for the consumers of Code Halos. For example, all major airlines may leverage similar amplifiers, provide common interfaces, and harvest similar Big Data sets. However, the algorithm and the way it is used can always be unique to the solution, and thus deliver proprietary insights and value. That's why it's important to devote considerable resources—in terms of attention, budget, and talent—to the development of the algorithm.

Facebook's EdgeRank Algorithm Makes It Personal

In September 2006, Facebook made one of its biggest and ultimately best bets by changing the application interface from the relatively static "wall" format to the more dynamic News Feed format. Facebook described the new interface this way:

> News Feed highlights what's happening in your social
> circles on Facebook. It updates a personalized list of
> news stories throughout the day, so you'll know when
> Mark adds Britney Spears to his Favorites or when your
> crush is single again. Now, whenever you log in, you'll
> get the latest headlines generated by the activity of your

friends and social groups.... These features are not only different from anything we've had on Facebook before, but they're quite unlike anything you can find on the web.[9]

At first, Facebook users were unimpressed. In fact, more than 100,000 customers logged complaints within the first 48 hours.[10] But Facebook did not back down—because its algorithms had validated that News Feed was the right move. The data showed how dedicated Facebook users had actually been using the site, and News Feed better enabled such usage. In other words, by managing trusted algorithms, the Facebook team knew its users—and their actual needs and wants—better than those users knew themselves.

The analysis was right. As Facebook rolled out News Feed more broadly and countered early negative views, users grew to like it. Facebook had about 12 million active users when it was introduced in 2006.[11] Just six years later, the number surpassed 1 billion.[12]

The "secret sauce" of News Feed is the EdgeRank algorithm, which has three main components:[13]

- **Affinity:** How close you are to the author of a post, determined by a proprietary affinity score.
- **Weight:** Photos get the most weight, followed by links and then plain text posts.
- **Time decay:** How fresh the post is.

By evaluating these components, EdgeRank delivers the right information, from the right people, in the right format, and at the right time to individual customers. It's what makes the Facebook experience—scrolling through the site to see what your friends are up to—so sticky and compelling.

EdgeRank proved to be a knockout blow to MySpace; it has also managed to keep more recent Facebook competitors, like Google+, at bay. Facebook users, who are already connected with their network of friends in a dynamic and compelling place, have so far shown little interest in going elsewhere for this type of experience.

Successful Algorithms Power Code Connections and Create Insight

All successful Code Halo algorithms, including EdgeRank, have three key attributes: they contextualize, individualize, and analyze.

- **Contextualize: Filter noise to map engagement to context.** Contextualizing challenges—asking the right questions, and viewing issues through the right set of lenses—is now a key determinant of commercial success. Clay Shirky is an author, consultant, and NYU professor who—as he puts it—"studies the effects of the Internet on society." He describes the challenges of managing in a Big Data world this way: "It's not information overload; it's filter failure" that can stop firms from succeeding.[14] The algorithm becomes that filter, and its proper creation starts with contextualization: What problem are we trying to solve? What's our set of hypotheses on meaningful correlations? Why will a customer find value in that? EdgeRank allows the Facebook team to contextualize what is most important to the typical user.

- **Individualize: Use algorithms to create an individual experience.** EdgeRank's central goal is to individualize the Facebook experience. Though most of us like to think that our wants, needs, and interests are unique to us, they rarely are. If we were so completely different, Google, Netflix, and Pandora wouldn't work. These companies know that certain people behave in similar patterns; but they use algorithms to focus on the most important of these attributes to create the sense of an individualized experience.

- **Analyze: Examine data to generate new insights.** Over time, successful algorithms allow for analysis of a business—either at the atomic level of an individual customer or product, or in terms of organizational units or market segments—with a level of precision and empiricism previously unavailable. With algorithms, the corporate strategy and planning sessions can mature from an exchange of opinion to a discussion based on the meritocracy of fact. Using a trusted algorithm like

EdgeRank meant that the Facebook product management teams could continually ascertain user behavior, ask better questions, and understand what behaviors or product features drive critical business outcomes. Over time, such analysis can turn hindsight into foresight, an understanding of predictive indicators and behaviors.

The most effective Code Halo algorithms enable such customization, individualization, and analysis. When utilized properly, the algorithms drive the management of Code Halos—and of the entire organization. When a management team sees how powerful these algorithm-derived insights are, they come to believe that making key decisions without them would be irresponsible.

All Data, Great and Small

Data is the fuel of Code Halos—a renewable resource increased via effective amplifiers, application interfaces used on a daily basis, and robust algorithms that help to make *business meaning*. Once these elements are successfully in place, a virtuous cycle of usage drives the constant generation of large amounts of data.

If your firm is not gobbling up computing memory and your IT staff is not making impassioned pleas for more resources, it is an indication that you may be missing the Code Halo movement.

As Pandora Co-founder Tim Westergren shared, "When you architect a product … you must ask, 'What within my product is going to allow me to collect data?' … for when you scale, the data at scale becomes key to you."[15]

Anatomy Lesson #3: You're gonna need a bigger boat.

Today, most IT organizations are not properly prepared for the coming onslaught of Big Data. Remember the crew's reaction in the movie *Jaws* when they first saw just how big the great white was? Many winning organizations are beginning to recognize that they're going to need a "bigger boat"—in terms of software, hardware, cloud-based  resources, and, most important, staff with data expertise, to create value from the coming orders-of-magnitude increases in data.

How much data is being collected today? Well, the word "big" in Big Data doesn't begin to cover it; "colossal" might be more fitting. We are currently generating enough data each day to fill the equivalent of 5.8 billion average-size PCs.[16] Fortunately, storage capacity is keeping pace. Today, a $300 device can store 3 terabytes of music—over a million MP3 songs.[17]

Start-up entrepreneurs, software developers, and large enterprises alike are wrestling with the opportunity that data represents. If your firm is not gobbling up computing memory and your IT staff is not making impassioned pleas for more resources (budget, staff, hardware, software, cloud-based storage), it is an indication that you may be missing the Code Halo movement.

Netflix Lassos Data to Win in the Market

The aggregate growth rate of Big Data is so overwhelming that it can be more instructive to consider Big Data in the context of an individual company. Netflix, a Code Halo winner with Big Data, has:[18]

- More than 25 million users.
- About 30 million plays per day (every rewind, fast forward, or pause is tracked).

- More than 2 billion hours of streaming video watched every three months.
- About 4 million ratings per day.
- About 3 million searches per day.
- Geo-location data.
- Device information.
- Metadata from third parties such as Nielsen.
- Social media data from Facebook and Twitter.

Big Data has enabled Netflix to continue to gain insights into its customers, highlighting new opportunities for the company. An example is the successful foray the company made into the world of original content in 2013.

Creating television programming and movies has historically been more art than science. Even at the most successful studios, it has been an exercise of trial and error. William Goldman, the Oscar-winning writer of *Butch Cassidy and the Sundance Kid* (among many other films), famously said of the movie-making business, "nobody knows anything."[19] HBO, which started airing original programming in the late 1970s, didn't win any Emmy Awards until the 1990s. Netflix, on the other hand, garnered 10 Emmy nominations in its first year of original programming, with nine of those nominations going to the drama *House of Cards*.[20] How did Netflix achieve in one year what it took HBO nearly 20 years to do? Was it luck—or was it because the Netflix team managed its original programming with Code Halos?

Just as the Facebook team used its Big Data and algorithms to determine that its News Feed feature would drive customer growth and retention, Netflix did the same with its creation of *House of Cards*, as was covered in *The New York Times*:

> In any business, the ability to see into the future is
> the killer app, and Netflix may be getting close with
> *House of Cards*. The series, directed by David Fincher,
> starring Kevin Spacey and based on a popular British
> series, is already the most streamed piece of content in

the United States and 40 other countries, according to Netflix. The spooky part about that? Executives at the company knew it would be a hit before anyone shouted "action."

Netflix, which has 27 million subscribers in the nation and 33 million worldwide, ran the numbers. It already knew that a healthy share had streamed the work of Mr. Fincher, the director of *The Social Network*, from beginning to end. And films featuring Mr. Spacey had always done well, as had the British version of *House of Cards*. With those three circles of interest, Netflix was able to find a Venn diagram intersection that suggested that buying the series would be a very good bet on original programming.

Big bets are now being informed by Big Data, and no one knows more about audiences than Netflix.[21,*]

An executive who asked not to be named in the article said this model would change the way the TV business operates. "… [I]t is clear that having a very molecular understanding of user data is going to have a big impact on how things happen in television," he said. Consider that phrase: *"a very molecular understanding"* of customer desires and product development.

Business history is littered with great and embarrassing guesses: the Ford Edsel, the Pontiac Aztek, New Coke, Kevin Costner's *Waterworld*, the Apple Newton—opinion-based creations that came at enormous financial and reputational cost. Now we're at the beginning of an era of management by empiricism, driven by the proper management of Code Halos. More on the "death of the HIPPO" later.[22]

New Business Models Showcase
Code Halo Value

While all of the elements we've already discussed are necessary, they're not *sufficient* for a solution to really take off. The final piece of the puzzle is the business model, which needs to make good business sense. The service or product can't just be "cool"; it must deliver significant cost savings, revenue generation, or even a new way to monetize a business process or customer interaction.

Many companies are exploring ways to establish pricing based on customer usage or behavior, and there are already new business models bringing Code Halo solutions to life.

- **Aligning costs to performance:** Insurance companies are linking insurance premiums to customers who behave in ways that reduce costs—such as driving without accidents or maintaining a home to prevent damage or liability claims. Healthcare providers can reward customers who break bad habits or actively work to maintain and improve their health. New motion sensors can detect smoking,[23] and companies are developing tooth sensors to help monitor eating habits as well as oral hygiene.[24]

- **Targeting the retail collision:** Square Wallet is an app designed to extend users' personal banking codes by connecting them with retail organizations at specific moments of engagement. The technology enables a seamless, secure exchange of funds for a good or service via a mobile device. Users simply open Square Wallet, check in to the business they're visiting, and say their name at checkout to have their card charged automatically. It rewards customers with convenience at the point of sale, lowers labor costs, provides a rich stream of business analytics data, and creates a stickier customer relationship for retailers.[25]

- **Monitoring and reporting:** Smart meters that monitor and report on utilities usage are offering potential savings to customers. They can also deliver more predictability for power generation and distribution processes.[26]

- **Customer influence:** Multiple commercial models in the life sciences space are already being affected or will soon be reshaped by Code Halo solutions. Storage provider EMC recently reported how interactions with physicians, sales and marketing activities, and consumers are improving as a result. For example, outcome-based commercial models are aligning payments to results, and healthcare providers are using social and mobile technologies to better engage patients.[27]

- **Building the personal code asset:** Imagine if a major retailer or bank could have the information needed to build relationships with members of certain demographic groups in specific metropolitan areas such as Boston or London. Companies like Personal and Yes Profile are doing just this by helping their customers add data that is meaningful to specific types of businesses to their Code Halos.[28] Yes Profile and Personal both allow people to create—and then sell—a record of selected personal data. As models like this proliferate and mature, the exchange of personal consumer data will be more valuable than any specific transaction.

The list of such business model innovations goes on and on. Some of these ideas have already changed an industry or key process, while other solutions have yet to be proven. But whether you are a seasoned executive, entrepreneur, business student, line-of-business owner, technology leader, investor, or merely an interested observer, thinking about the commercial model is essential to building—or buying, or partnering with—a Code Halo solution that really sings in the market.

Why Didn't They Tune in the Zune?

Even if you get the amplifier, interface, and algorithms right, an initiative can still fail without the proper business model. Take the Microsoft Zune for example. Following Apple's iPod success, Microsoft, in late 2006, brought its considerable muscle to the portable media device sector with the Zune. However, the company called it quits and discontinued the Zune by 2011. How could this happen?

As a Code Halo amplifier, the Zune was *technically* as good as or even superior to all MP3 players, including the iPod, on the market at the time. In 2007, a 32GB Zune HD cost $289. Apple's competing iPod Touch with 32GB retailed for $299. The Zune had a more intuitive look and feel, radio capability, significantly better video output, longer battery life, and the choice of five colors instead of one.

The application interface for the Zune, the Zune Music Pass, was elegant, intuitive, and visually on par with Apple's iTunes. And the company had a powerful, fully integrated marketing program behind the initiative. Bill Gates was personally involved, and the company enlisted armies of Zune-masters on college campuses.[29] Yet it all ended in tears.

The Zune fell woefully short on experience beauty, because Microsoft had not worked through the entire business model. It failed to build the proper partnerships—in the form of third-party music licensing and software applications—to deliver a seamless user experience. By contrast, Apple concentrated on developing relationships with partners, thereby creating a beautiful end-to-end user experience. In addition to licensing, Apple started building the music and app ecosystem from 1999 onward, so by 2007 the iPod had 75,000 apps and 21,000 games available. The Zune? Nine apps and seven games!

The Zune violated one of the fundamental principles of competing on Code Halos: it **generated no information** and was therefore unable to deliver a meaningful user experience. This was beyond unacceptable to MP3 aficionados who rejected the Zune because it could not deliver that "Wow, they're reading my mind!" feeling. College students stared at their Zune-masters, with a "You've got to be kidding me" look. To them, using the Zune was like walking into a fabulously designed new restaurant that had no food available. Without the full experience, Microsoft had created just one more MP3 player—a basic hardware device with a goofy name.

Apple, by contrast, created both a stunning machine and a compelling experience through a full business ecosystem—one that indeed *made meaning*. Not only did the iPod make listening to music enjoyable, but it also led to new discoveries—of new types of music, of new ways and places to listen, and of how to enjoy other forms of media as well.

Anatomy Lesson #4: Don't Zune out.

How did Microsoft fail so badly with Zune? The company utilized massive resources—in R&D, design, development, distribution, and marketing—in creating its intended iPod killer. Microsoft also did a terrific job in getting the amplifier, interface, algorithms, and Big Data right. But because it got the business model wrong, the entire initiative became an embarrassing failure. So, don't Zune out. Ensure you have a business model that will make your Code Halo a commercial success.

Balance Focus on Five Components for a Winning Solution

All successful Code Halos contain the five key elements—the amplifier, interface, algorithms, Big Data, and a supporting business model—which are built-to-purpose and work in harmony. Whatever your Code Halo solution, it should also adhere to the four anatomy lessons:

- If it costs more than $50, and you can't eat it, put a Code Halo around it.
- Algorithms are the foundation of experience.
- You're gonna need a bigger boat for all of that data.
- Don't Zune out.

Now that we've discussed what a Code Halo is, and the key elements of a Code Halo solution—including the creation of new business models—we'll take a deeper look at the SMAC Stack: the underlying foundation of Code Halo solutions.

CHAPTER FIVE

The SMAC Stack:
The New Technology of Code

We've mentioned how the consumer technology revolution of the past decade has been enabled by four key technologies that work in combination: social, mobile, analytics, and cloud, or "SMAC" for short. In this chapter, we will explore in more detail how and why the SMAC Stack is so key in the development of the Code Halo phenomenon.

Components of the SMAC Stack are the raw materials of Code Halos. They include:

- **Social technologies:** Blogs, wikis, email, instant messaging, social network services, and software applications that foster and facilitate interpersonal communications, both personal and business.
- **Mobile technologies:** From portable hardware devices—such as smartphones, tablets, wearables, personal digital assistants (PDAs), and global positioning systems (GPS)—to the software, applications, and networks that support and enable robust anywhere/anytime connectivity.
- **Analytics technologies:** These provide new levels of empiricism and insight by establishing a software supply chain of collecting, organizing, managing, measuring, analyzing, and reporting large amounts of disparate data on an ongoing basis.
- **Cloud computing:** This allows remotely based computing resources—such as servers, databases, and applications—to be delivered via the Internet (instead of being owned and hosted internally), allowing for flexibility of resources and, in many cases, much lower cost.

In the coming five years, organizations of all sizes must develop a mastery of SMAC technologies. But that's easier said than done. How can you make sense of this new wave of technology to seize competitive advantage? To address these questions, this chapter provides: (1) a historical perspective on corporate computing to see where and how the SMAC model fits today; (2) an overview of current SMAC technologies, and of how pervasive this new model has become; and (3) a view of how the SMAC model is already upending several established industries.

Mastering the Fifth Wave of Corporate IT

SMAC technologies are laying the foundation for a new master corporate IT architecture. There have been four master technology architectures in the corporation over the past 50 years: the mainframe, the minicomputer, Client/Server, and the Internet. Each of these eras lasted roughly a decade or more and (as outlined by the "S" curves in Figure 5.1) drove business productivity higher during those periods. The new SMAC curve will produce even greater levels of productivity and value during the next years.

Catching the Fifth Wave of Corporate IT

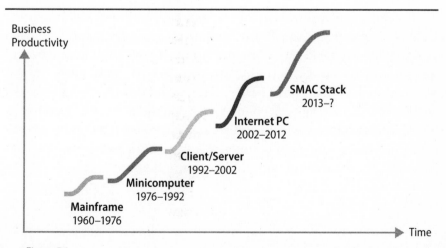

Figure 5.1

Driving Business Value Through New Technologies

Each of the previous four architectures found success by focusing on key business processes and supporting "killer" technology applications (such as the general ledger with the mainframe, Enterprise Resource Planning (ERP) with Client/Server, and eCommerce with the Internet) to drive new levels of value. The waves are represented as "S" curves, since the business productivity these technology models created—in either cost savings, revenue generation, or productivity gains—would form an S shape over time. Initially (at the bottom left of an S curve) a new technology model would drive few productivity gains, as the internal IT organization was learning how to implement the new platform and there was little integration with key business processes. Once the new technology platform was applied to key processes or business functions, business productivity would shoot skyward. However, early productivity gains waned once those architectures were in place—and investments reached points of diminishing returns (which is why the top of each "S" goes flat.) After all, once you've put your ERP backbone in place, you don't need a second one.

Today, it's clear we are at the top of the fourth curve and starting to jump to the fifth. As with other "curve jumps," this shift will generate significant dislocation and wealth creation on the supply (or vendor) side of the industry—across hardware, software, and services sectors—and drive new levels of productivity on the demand (or user) side of the industry.

But there are two reasons why it will happen faster and at a larger scale this time. First, the SMAC technology model is already proven at scale, for unlike the mainframe, minicomputer, and Client/Server waves—which started in the enterprise—SMAC was born, raised, and matured in the consumer market. In many ways, much of the architecture is in place. Second, as we highlight on the next page, SMAC technologies—which were previously powerful but disconnected consumer tools—are now coming together in an integrated stack to produce a higher order of business benefits in the enterprise.

SMAC as a Technology Stack: No Technology Is an Island

One key to understanding and knowing what to do about this transition is in viewing these technologies as an integrated whole. Imagine your smartphone without its apps, disconnected from the Web, the cloud, and your personal networks. On its own, it would be a very expensive pocket watch. Its power and value only come when the SMAC technologies work in harmony.

The same is true in a corporate setting. Over the past few years, the potential of the discrete "piece parts" of this new technology architecture have been hyped to the hilt. However, the *combination of these technologies* into an integrated stack is what drives true business value, as together they have a multiplier effect (e.g., mobile inputs continually driving analytics).

This phenomenon is similar to the early days of the Client/Server wave. In the late 1980s and early 1990s, various components of the Client/Server architecture—such as relational databases, Ethernet networks, Unix operating systems, and PCs—were all commercially available. While technical experts recognized the superiority of these piece parts over existing technologies, user companies realized little business gain when they implemented the elements in stand-alone fashion. Only when Client/Server technologies were implemented as a stack aligned as solutions for key functions such as sales, finance, and HR—with PCs atop Unix servers, connected over networks and tapping into relational databases—did the architecture take hold.

Today, we are experiencing an important parallel between this 1990s trend and the current SMAC technology stack. With Client/Server technologies, enterprise applications—such as ERP, CRM, and Human Resource Management (HRM)—became the organizing constructs that drove business value through the Client/Server stack. Today, the organizing construct for the SMAC Stack is the Code Halo. Without such a focus, the majority of SMAC technology implementations—such as "Bring your own device" or "Let's move to the cloud"—become merely "technology for technology's sake" and therefore generate little bottom-line value.

A Step Change Driving Exponential Growth in Computing Devices and Data

By any definition, this market shift is occurring faster—and at dramatically greater scale—than prior technology shifts. For example:

- Corporations will spend $360 billion per year on SMAC hardware, software, and services by 2016.[1]
- More than 75 billion devices will be connected to the Web by 2020.[2]
- By 2020, corporations will be managing 50 times the data currently managed.[3]

With each wave of corporate IT, the number of computers worldwide has increased by roughly an order of magnitude, and the data generated has grown at an even faster rate. In looking back at the previous four master IT architectures—and understanding the dynamics of the transitions between architectures—we begin to recognize that the speed and scale of the coming transition will greatly outstrip prior shifts. Let's look at each of the master technology architectures through a simple lens of the number of devices and the amount of data being managed.

- **Mainframe era: 100,000 computers.** This market, dominated by IBM, topped out at roughly 100,000 computers worldwide. This was a combination of the approximately 15,000 mainframes installed at the height of this era and all of the ancillary computing devices (remember the green screens?) attached to these machines.[4]
- **Minicomputer era: Millions of computers, 2.6 exabytes of data.** This era ushered in a trend of smaller, departmental computers called "minis," which is ironic by today's standard, since the 1.5-pound iPad has significantly more processing power than the 750-pound DEC VAX of 1980 had. At the end of the minicomputer era, 91 companies were making minicomputers, and one of the most popular models—the DEC PDP-11—had sold a total of 600,000 units. About 2.6

exabytes of data were under management by the minis. (To put this in perspective, one exabyte is 1 million terabytes and can store the equivalent of approximately 100,000 times all the printed material in the U.S. Library of Congress.)[5]

- **Client/Server era: 100 million computers, 15.8 exabytes of data.** The early 1990s brought another order of magnitude of growth in enterprise computers with new market leaders such as Microsoft, SAP, Oracle, Cisco, and EMC. Once PCs, Unix boxes, and network routers were installed to run the new enterprise software, more than 100 million computers had been sold, with 15.8 exabytes of data in the associated databases.[6]

- **Internet era: 1 billion computers, 54.5 exabytes of data.** Connectivity to an entire new generation of devices and users drove the number of desktop and—increasingly—laptop computers worldwide to 1 billion and tripled data under management to 54.5 exabytes.[7]

- **SMAC Stack: 10 billion computers, 1,800 exabytes of data.** The number of devices is now nearly 10 billion but quickly on its way to 100 billion, and data volume is growing to 35,000 exabytes by 2020 (more than 600 times the data under management at the end of the Internet era).[8]

The Rapid Growth of the SMAC Computing Model

This massive leap in computing devices and data under management will occur in two steps in the next several years. The first step—the mobility movement—will be driven by the billions of smart devices in the hands of the world's population. The second step—that will take these numbers to remarkably high levels—will be the Internet of Things movement, driven by 100 billion devices mostly in the "hands" of machines.

Mobility and Analytics Lead the Way

We will soon cross the line where there are more computers on Earth than people. If this number seems overstated to you, simply take inventory of the smartphones, tablets, PCs, and gaming consoles in your home ... then take inventory of your work-related devices.

Consider this: "Today your smartphone has more computing power than existed in all of NASA in 1969."[9]

And yet all you do is play Angry Birds.

In all seriousness—we are very close to full market saturation when it comes to mobile adoption. You should assume by this point that any customer to whom you want to sell or any talented employee you wish to hire is carrying a sophisticated smart device at all times. What's now important is not *who* has a smart device, but *what* they are doing with it. They're already doing a lot, and this will only accelerate over time. For example:

- By 2017, mobile network data will exceed fixed network data by 300%.[10]
- Over 100 billion mobile apps will be downloaded in 2013; over 200 billion downloads are predicted by 2015.[11,12]
- Mobile apps will grow from a $6 billion industry today to a $55.7 billion industry by 2015.[13]
- The number of smartphone shipments is expected to be 1 billion in 2016.[14]
- The iPhone 5 sold 5 million units after its first weekend on the market in September 2012.[15]
- There were approximately 200,000 Android Market apps available in May 2011. By October 2013, there were over 850,000.[16,17]
- Globally, mobile data traffic will increase 18-fold between 2011 and 2016, reaching 10.8 exabytes per month by 2016.[18]

By any statistic or definition, it's now a mobile world. The question is, where will it lead us—or where will we lead *it?* We've seen the following three-step process take shape in enterprise mobility adoption in our work with clients over the past several years:

1. **Mobile-enabling existing applications:** This step—which some people term "putting lipstick on the pig"—is necessary and nontrivial. Most companies have dozens, if not hundreds, of applications that they designed to run on desktop or laptop computers that their customers now need to access via smartphones and tablets. The redesign of the user interface—along with important security and performance concerns—multiplied across dozens of internal systems and myriad third-party mobile devices makes this ongoing effort a difficult necessity.

2. **Transforming key business processes:** Many organizations are now realizing that they need to reconfigure, if not entirely reengineer, core business processes due to the rise of mobility. For example, many processes simply used to assume that key participants—whether employees or customers—would engage in their work in **one physical place** during defined business hours. Now that those constraints have been removed, and people can work anytime from anywhere, companies are forced to rethink many fundamentals. (We discuss the new norms of working in the digital age in Chapter 10.)

3. **Creating new business models:** Mobility is also prompting people to reconsider some long-accepted business models. For example, many retail banks are rethinking the role of the local branch in a world of mobility. We have seen several independent studies that highlight a similar issue for banks in both North America and Europe: they could close half of their retail branches and actually increase revenues. Mobility is driving this process of "creative destruction" in which organizations are looking at large portions of established business models with new eyes.

Data, data everywhere—but analytics needed to think! If you feel overwhelmed by information, you should; it means you're paying attention. Your organization may be feeling the strain of such data management—but given that today's data requirements will be a fraction of those of several years hence, there's no choice but to become proficient with such levels.

Data, data everywhere—but analytics needed to think!

This explosion of data is being driven by the SMAC Stack in two stages: human-generated and machine-generated.

Growth in Human-Generated Data

All of us, collectively hunched over our computers and smart devices, are expanding the universe of data—and several phenomena are accelerating this growth:

- **Behavioral analytics:** It's no longer good enough to capture the transaction in your systems (e.g., "Joe bought a hammer for $9.99 on October 25"). Now it's vitally important to understand *why* this transaction occurred, and what associated transactions occurred as a result. In other words: What is the before, during, and after involved in any transaction? Companies must gain very specific views on the variables that drive their customers', employees', and business partners' key behaviors.

- **Social networking:** The growth of mobile devices and social networks means that your systems are constantly being hit by suppliers, customers, and employees across your entire value chain as we discussed in Chapter 3. Individuals are talking openly about your company, in an "anytime, anywhere" fashion. Organizations, in response, are developing "social listening centers" to tap into user profiles and conversations across generic social sites such as Google, Twitter, Facebook, and LinkedIn, as well as more industry-specific or demographic-specific social sites. It's not only necessary to track and store this data; you must then tie it to key corporate processes or initiatives, such as a product launch or new marketing campaign to gain new insights on corporate performance.

- **System of record:** Big Data is not just about the SMAC Stack. Classic legacy systems are also generating more data than ever, either through direct output or abstracted output that is captured in data warehouses and business intelligence systems.

- **Cloud-based applications:** Your organization is also generating rapidly increasing amounts of data out in the cloud, through multiple SaaS applications (like Salesforce.com, Workday, and Concur.) This can present its own challenges; it's your company's data, yet it's sitting elsewhere.

While this human-generated data is growing exponentially, such growth is nothing compared to what's just around the corner with machine-generated data.

Smart Cars, Smart Houses, Smart Grids, Smart Health: The Coming Explosion in Machine-Generated Data

Today, each layer of the SMAC Stack is experiencing outsized growth. However, things will get *really* interesting by the end of 2015 as the SMAC Stack becomes the staging area for another much more profound leap in the scale and ubiquity of computing: the Internet of Things that we first introduced in Chapter 3.[19]

We touched on a few examples earlier, and here's another that involves something you probably already own: think of your next car as a truly connected device, with many of its systems online. Whether next-generation GPS systems, streaming of music to the dashboard, or real-time engine diagnostics, multiple core systems will be online and continually transmitting data via the Internet. In fact, the car may even *drive itself.*

Additionally, your car will not be in isolation. It could be connected to your calendaring system, and automatically notify whoever you are driving to meet if you are 15 minutes late. It will communicate with your home security and air conditioning systems on your way home, so that the house is open, properly lit, and at the temperature you like when you arrive.

Outfitting everyday machines with sensing technologies and connecting them to the Internet will be the largest contributor to data growth in the next decade—and will occur in three primary categories:

1. **Consumer scale:** Cars, appliances, video games, homes, sporting equipment, etc.
2. **Industrial scale:** Power generators, locomotives, airplanes, trucks, security systems, etc.
3. **Societal scale:** Power grids, water systems, earthquake detection, traffic management, etc.

Such machine-to-machine-to-human connectivity will have a profound impact on the consumer and home experience, as well as transportation systems, retail, industrial supply chains, energy grids, security, and public safety. Retailers will be able to provide precision retailing at minimal cost. Manufacturers of complex products can provide preemptive maintenance. Doctors will be able to use remote care to stay in regular contact with postsurgical patients, remotely monitoring their key vital signs and recommending recuperative steps in real time. Similarly, farmers will "watch" livestock via embedded sensors, determining illnesses, pregnancies, or even stress in their animals. The use cases are myriad and promise to create rapid dislocation in industry after industry.[20]

The Business Impact of SMAC: The Value Chain Is Becoming "Unchained"

Though you may feel like you've seen lots of hype around cloud computing and social media, the impact of this new technology stack on the corporation is currently being *underhyped*. SMAC Stack technologies are not simply being "glued onto" the traditional corporate model; in many cases, they are creating an *entirely new model*. This is an important distinction between the SMAC Stack model and the Client/Server model. At their most fundamental, the 1990s Client/Server systems made an industrial business model more efficient and effective. These enterprise applications allowed for better management of products or people. As such, IT leaders during this time didn't need to engage in true business model innovation; instead, they needed to **apply new computing models** to **established ways** of doing business.

The SMAC Stack, by contrast, is a **new** technology model *creating new business models*. In the same manner that steam power, steel, and electricity provided the platform for the industrial corporate model, the new technology stack is providing the foundation for the knowledge corporate model.

SMAC Stack technologies are not simply being "glued onto" the traditional corporate model; in many cases, they are creating an entirely new model.

Take, for instance, how Craigslist has transformed newspaper ads. As recently as 10 years ago, classified ads represented one of the primary revenue streams for newspapers in the United States, generating $19.6 billion in revenues in 2000.[21] By 2012, that figure had dropped to less than $5 billion.[22] Where did many of those classified ads go? To Craigslist, where each month more than 80 million new ads are posted to an audience of more than 60 million unique visitors. And this is all managed by a grand total of about 40 people in the Craigslist headquarters in San Francisco.[23]

For decades, newspapers had managed this information-intensive activity as an industrial process, with the very expensive co-location of people, process, and tools. This industrial process was replicated—

sometimes multiple times—at hundreds of newspapers across the country, employing tens of thousands of people in local markets ... and it was eviscerated in just a few years by a few dozen people with origins in a different industry.

By no means is this story isolated to newspapers. Another example of the efficiency and disruption of a business model based on the SMAC Stack is highlighted by the metrics of 11-year-old Wikipedia vs. the 244-year-old Encyclopedia Britannica. The table in Figure 5.2 reveals the incredible scale advantages of the SMAC-Stack-powered Wikipedia.

The Transformation of Knowledge (Rule, Wikipedia!)[24]

	Encyclopedia Britannica	Wikipedia
Year founded	1768	2001
Articles	65,000	4,355,223
Languages	1	271
Words	40 million	2 billion
Updated	Annually	Real-time
Mistakes per article	2.92	3.86
Cost	$729	Free

Figure 5.2

Small wonder that Encyclopedia Britannica published its last physical version in early 2012.

Craigslist and Wikipedia stand as extreme yet simple examples of dematerialization (the process by which material-based value chains go virtual.) How many similar knowledge-based processes—now incorrectly structured and managed as industrial processes—exist in your organization?

Don't Get SMACked

SMAC Stack technologies are not only the raw materials of Code Halos, but they also represent the coming dominant model of corporate computing. These technologies will reach unprecedented levels of scope and scale, being infused directly in products and services and greatly altering core business processes and, in some cases, entire industry structures. In Chapter 6, we provide an overview of the Crossroads Model, through which you can determine the state of your own industry's digital transformation.

Later, in Chapter 11, we will discuss practical approaches for organizing your IT function to seize these transformational opportunities.

CHAPTER SIX

The Pattern of Digital Disruption: The Crossroads Model

At this point, you've read about your personal Code Halo, the five types of business Code Halos, the transformational power of the SMAC Stack and, if you're like the hundreds of managers and executives we've consulted with on this topic, you are probably now wondering exactly how and where these concepts may apply to your organization.

Finding a starting point for this analysis is easier said than done. External issues such as your industry structure, the nature of your products and/or services, and your customer base's demographics will all have an impact on your potential next steps. You also have to consider what your competitors may, or may not, be up to. Internal factors will also play a role. Does your organization have a culture that supports change? Does your firm have a strong IT team with the right capabilities? And even if you see the opportunity and build a compelling vision, can your organization execute against it?

To answer these questions, we developed the Crossroads Model, which is based on our consulting work with many leading companies and our research findings. The model stems from our recognition of the pattern of how Code Halos emerge inside companies, and how those firms successfully deploy them. We saw how organizations all followed a similar path. We also looked at Code Halo failures, attempting to ascertain what went wrong, and the pattern surfaced again.

The Crossroads Model emerged as a diagnostic tool to determine where a particular industry or organization might be in this journey, and what the appropriate steps are to take. In Part III of the book, we provide specific implementation recommendations in line with the model.

The Five Stages of the Crossroads Model

The Crossroads Model has five distinct stages. Before we get to the individual stages, we must first highlight a key point of the model: the rise of certain Code Halo leaders seemed to occur "overnight." However, much like certain entertainers, these overnight successes were actually years in the making. As exhibited in the model below, initiatives often need to incubate for extended periods—usually several years—during the first three stages of the model. Yet, when built properly and introduced at the right time, these virtualized business models can scale drastically and quickly in impact and scope.

The Crossroads Model: Winning with Code Halos

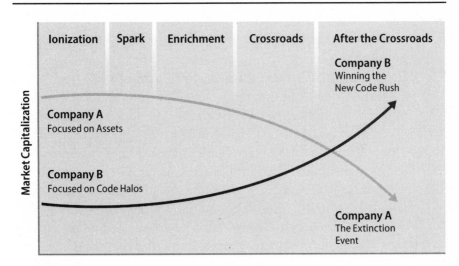

| Ionization | Spark | Enrichment | Crossroads | After the Crossroads |

Company B
Winning the New Code Rush

Market Capitalization

Company A
Focused on Assets

Company B
Focused on Code Halos

Company A
The Extinction Event

Figure 6.1

The stages of the Crossroads Model are:

1. **Ionization: A fertile context for innovation.** There may not be any Code Halos of note in your industry at this stage, but the context for their introduction is ripe. We call this

"Ionization," for the conditions are similar to those in nature when lightning is about to strike. They often include the right alignment of economic pressures, enhanced customer expectations, and new technologies, allowing a Code Halo to seem a natural or obvious solution. As examples, the mobile phone industry went through Ionization in 2005, and the customer interface in retail banking is in this phase today.

2. **The Spark: Where Code Halos emerge in an industry.** The "Spark" is when a Code Halo initiative is introduced as a pilot. It's similar to lighting a match; in the right context, a small spark can catch and turn into a blaze, but in the wrong context, it can quickly burn out. The Spark phase is necessary for the proper launch of a Code Halo—ensuring the technology, associated processes, organization, business model, and customer value proposition are aligned. If done correctly, the Spark catches—Code Halos build, associated algorithms are also developed, new ideas and offerings are then created, and associated processes evolve to support the virtual as well as the physical.

3. **Enrichment: When the Code Halo solutions scale.** In this stage the Code Halo starts to scale rapidly in both its number of users and amount of data generated. Initially, the Enrichment phase can also create dissonance inside your organization. Though your technical staff will be enthused to see the new technologies grab hold, your business-oriented teams will not see meaningful business results quite yet. However, Enrichment is vitally important. Code Halo initiatives can enter the stage as nascent initiatives yet exit it—usually between 18 and 36 months later—as core differentiating capabilities. For example, the movie rental business entered the Enrichment stage in 2004 as Netflix's Cinematch engine was taking hold.

4. **The Crossroads: Where markets flip.** This is a compressed period of time—often between one and three years—when industry leadership shifts. At the Crossroads, Code Halos have reached critical mass and created new customer expectations

and economic models. The business results that seemed so elusive during Spark and Enrichment begin to accrue very quickly. This drives the rapid and sometimes violent swing in reputation, revenue, and market value.

5. **After the Crossroads: Where both positive and negative momentum prove very difficult to stop.** After the Crossroads, the migration of value accelerates from one set of companies to another. Code Halo market leaders continue to gain customer attention in terms of both mind and market share, as well as investor attention (in terms of market valuation) at accelerated rates. On the other hand, the firms that missed the Code Halo "shift" find themselves on a very slippery slope as all business metrics increase in negative momentum. Famed hedge fund manager Jim Chanos has recognized this shift from an investor perspective.

> One of the differences in the value game now versus, say, 15 or 20 years ago, is that declining businesses, while they often throw off cash early in their decline, find that cash flow actually reaches a tipping point and goes negative much faster than it used to.... The advent of digitization in lots of businesses also means that the timing gets compressed ... you need to move quickly or you are road kill on the digital highway.[1]

The Crossroads Model Across Multiple Industries

The detailed trajectory will differ by industry, organization, and process, but the model looks the same across many sectors. For example, when Amazon went public in 1997 and its valuation soared as the Internet bubble was inflating, Borders and Barnes & Noble were collectively worth eight times the value of Amazon—with roughly 50 times its revenue and 100 times its customer base.

By 2005, Amazon was worth twice as much as Borders and Barnes & Noble combined, and had equaled both retailers' customer count (in the same book, movie, and music retailing markets) and associated revenues. Just five years later, Amazon was worth 100 times more than

Borders and Barnes & Noble combined, and Borders had declared bankruptcy (see Figure 6.2).

Bookselling at the Crossroads

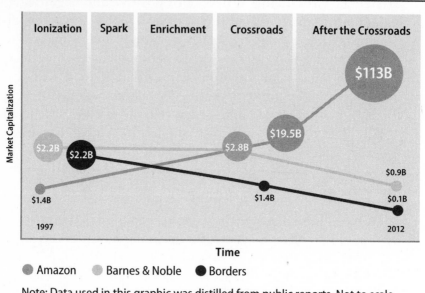

Note: Data used in this graphic was distilled from public reports. Not to scale.

Figure 6.2

Similar dynamics have marked the transformation of the mobile phone market. The dominant player of the late 1990s and early 2000s, Nokia, has been replaced by organizations less focused on hardware features and more attuned to the Code Rules of a digitized marketplace (see Figure 6.3). We can observe this pattern consistently across more than a dozen industries to date.

Mobile Devices at the Crossroads

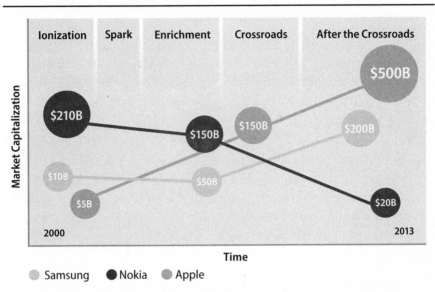

Note: Data used in this graphic was distilled from public reports. Not to scale.

Figure 6.3

Traditional Organizations Are Coming to the Crossroads

As shown in Figures 6.2 and 6.3 one industry after another has seen incumbents overtaken by new, highly digitized players. However, one of our key conclusions—and a central motivation for writing this book—is that many traditional organizations are likely to be caught off guard unless decision-makers recognize and adapt to the Crossroads Model.

Next, we outline the stages of the Crossroads Model in more detail.

Stage 1: The Ionizing Environment: Sense, Innovate, and Prepare to Pilot

Think of what the air feels and smells like before a storm arrives, just prior to a lightning strike. You sense it before seeing it or being able to describe it. Your hair may stand on end. The conditions—climate, humidity, static build—create the right environment for the release of an electrical charge.

Business leaders feel that same kind of electrified atmosphere when they sense that something—a challenge or an opportunity—is imminent. The major forces that companies everywhere are grappling with—globalization, economic volatility, a new mindset for problem solving, SMAC Stack technologies—are creating just such a charged or ionized context. The signals of a looming disruption are always the same:

- **Green shoots emerge.** Early examples of fresh ideas, such as a start-up or a new technology, begin to take root and gain traction. Major buzz surrounds a small, insignificant competitor that seemingly poses no threat to much bigger corporations. We see this today with companies such as Square in mobile banking and Waze in GPS.

- **Established competitors announce an "odd" technical initiative.** Your large competitors announce a product, service, or entry into an adjacent market that doesn't make immediate sense. But they're as smart as you are, so it's unwise to presume they are making a mistake. UPS's Delivery Information Acquisition Device (DIAD), or Allstate's Drivewise, are investments that look reasonable now, but seemed to some observers to be wild flights of fancy when they were first introduced.

- **There are no big signposts up ahead.** There will not be a mountain of data or a cohort of analysts to "prove" a shift is imminent. Market researchers and observers generally focus on the rear-view mirror more than the road ahead—which means that you'll "feel" the shift before there is data to prove anything.

- **Customer experiences in related industries have hit the Crossroads.** Code Halos in related industries change the expectation that customers, employees, and supply chain partners have of your company. Customers who have become accustomed to the ways of the "digital natives" get fed up with the ATM that doesn't know what language they speak or by the car that is dumber than their smartphone.

Many of these subtle, and not so subtle, signs are observable in many industries and business processes today, and the electric charge is strengthening. Our research has uncovered the following attributes that indicate a high likelihood of Ionization:

- **Knowledge-based businesses:** Industries in which the majority of revenue originates from knowledge-based products and services (e.g., financial services, media and entertainment, life sciences, healthcare, news and information services, large portions of retail) are undergoing Ionization more quickly. These industry "supply chains" are, in truth, already knowledge chains with high levels of information intensity.

- **Product businesses with "daily use" machines:** Manufacturers of machines that people use on a daily basis are Code Halo-enabling their products. These range from simple household appliances—a toothbrush, pill dispenser, or refrigerator—to more sophisticated consumer products: home HVAC systems, home security systems, and automobiles. This daily use rule also applies to the majority of machines in the industrial arena.

- **High Millennial concentration:** These are typically businesses in which a majority of customers and/or employees are 35 years of age or younger. Because Millennials grew up online, they view virtual experiences and interactions as being as "real" as physical ones. These customers and employees have little use for business models that do not keep up with their technical expectations.

- **Geographically distributed businesses:** Business models that transcend geographical boundaries with relative ease have digitized faster. Industries where employees can move work around internationally—where the core work processes are fluid and knowledge-based—have shown the ability to transform more quickly to a digital model.

- **Core offer commoditization:** When the "what" a customer purchases becomes standardized, the "how" they purchase and interact with it is open for change. This was a common element with books, music, maps, travel, and movies, and is clearly in play in portions of financial services, consumer goods, media and entertainment, manufacturing, and retail.

- **Well-defined regulatory environment:** It's commonly said that "innovation doesn't like regulation." Actually, that's not fully accurate. In reality, innovation doesn't like *potentially changing* regulation. As such, markets with stable regulatory environments are riper for innovation.

If your business is experiencing several of the items on the above list, your organization may well be experiencing Ionization. We see industry leaders in today's environment responding to Ionization situations in a variety of ways:

- Banking decision-makers are wrestling with wealth management solutions for up-and-coming Millennials.[2]
- Healthcare providers know their customer satisfaction ratings are subpar; many of them feel like Goliath waiting to be whacked by David's deadly rock.[3]
- Pharmaceutical companies see that selling wellness is more valuable to customers *and to them* than selling pills and treatments.

These leaders are not playing for short-term payoffs. They know the business atmosphere is ionized for transformative change, and they realize they must take steps now to win in the long term. Chances are that you too can feel Ionization occurring in your market. It's all about sensing change, recognizing where Code Halo solutions can emerge— and then piloting your own.

Stage 2: Create a Spark: Develop Your Best Code Halo Solutions

What occurred during Ionization is important, but it is only the first step. The Spark provides the tangible proof that an opportunity can come to life within your organization and market. To date, most initial Code Halo projects for companies are customer facing, either as customer-focused or product-focused solutions. It's during this period that the matching of an individual customer's likes, interests, location, and demographic information combines with a corporate halo. The relationship immediately transcends that of buyer/seller and becomes one of mutual interest and discovery. And it quickly becomes apparent whether such an initiative will take off or flounder.

Igniting a Spark is not easy, but businesses do it every day. The challenge is determining which Spark among the countless possibilities for improving the customer experience or internal processes will most benefit your business.

The insurance industry provides a good example. Progressive Insurance, for example, was founded in 1937 and grew steadily. In the late 1990s, company leadership recognized that the property and casualty insurance industry was in a state of Ionization and the environment was primed for simple ideas that could result in huge business payoffs. Progressive was among the first insurers to use the Internet to provide policy information and carrier rate comparisons. It focused assiduously on customer experience, offering services such as connecting customers with their body shops of choice.[4]

Focusing on the customer experience and using new technologies to improve service may seem quaint in retrospect, but Progressive recognized early on how Code Halos, applied across its value chain (customer and repair shop interactions, organizational information), could fundamentally change its operating model.

Igniting a Spark is not easy, but businesses do it every day. The challenge is determining which Spark among the countless possibilities for improving the customer experience or internal processes will most benefit your business.

Stage 3: Enrich and Scale at Internet Speed: Turn a Spark into a Blaze

Little may appear to be happening after the Spark of a new idea. Your CEO may ask, "How has this improved our customer satisfaction metrics?" Your CFO may inquire, "When will this initiative boost the bottom line?" You're likely to answer these questions by looking down at your shoes and replying meekly, "It hasn't moved the needle on those metrics … yet." This often creates tension for senior leaders who have placed a big bet on a telematics device, a crowdsourced product design, or a mobile app.

During the beginning of the Enrichment phase, questions about quantifiable results are initially difficult to answer (though we will provide some ideas in Chapter 12). Yet, the goal during this period is not to drive *immediately measurable* results (although that would be fantastic). Managers who focus too early on "moving the needle" with "metrics that matter" can slow the Enrichment process—and sometimes stop it entirely. The goal of Enrichment is to **build meaningful services and solutions** based on Code Halos. Once this is achieved, those much-sought-after results will follow at the Crossroads.

So despite the lack of quantifiable results, two very important things occur during this stage:

- **Code Halos "inflate" with information from a steadily growing number of interactions.** The Pandora user listens for several hours a week, each time offering more likes and dislikes. Athletes wearing Nike+ FuelBands work out each day around the world, generating more and more data. Pandora's and Nike's algorithms therefore become more robust, sophisticated, and fine-tuned.

- **Commercial models begin to emerge.** Key processes either become radically more efficient, or are altered in a fundamental manner to provide more value to customers, employees, and/or business partners. These changes are accompanied by new commercial models aligned more to creating and distributing knowledge and insight than physical products.

Google could not function as it does without having people conduct searches every day. Like a hot-air balloon that runs out of fuel, Google's PageRank algorithm "deflates" if people do not use it.[5] Google Research Director Peter Norvig offered insight into the idea of Enrichment (as well as Google's source of competitive advantage) when he said, "We don't have better algorithms. We just have more data."[6]

During the Enrichment period, a company gradually moves away from the mechanistic brokering of company/customer interactions, finds insights within the rich streams of data about customers, processes, partners, and devices, and starts to convert them into business value. For example, the years 2004 to 2007 marked a period of Enrichment for Apple. iTunes grew slowly, creating a foundation for the massive growth that would come later. In 2010, 10 billion songs were downloaded. Eighteen months later that figure had doubled to 20 billion.[7] Facebook followed a similar pattern of explosive growth, taking several years to reach 100 million users in 2008, then adding, on average, 100 million more users every 167 days. It reached 1 billion users late in 2012.[8]

Apple and Facebook took their time getting smarter and building user communities, which ultimately proved Code Halos' value. However, their business practices were not yet validated by financial results or other standard corporate metrics in the early days of the Enrichment phase.

Stage 4: The Crossroads: Where Markets Flip

"There are decades where nothing happens; and then there are weeks where decades happen."

—Vladimir Lenin

Industries and companies positioned at the Crossroads experience massive transition. Even though the industry may essentially look the same as it has for some time—after all, bookselling still involves some form of the "book"—the **basis of competition** has fundamentally changed. What customers expect—regarding their relationship with your company and their interactions with its products or services—shifts. The way investors reward your company's performance changes dramatically. In many cases, even the basic measures of financial performance—such as revenue per employee, gross margins, and return on capital—no longer look the same.

At the Crossroads, complex algorithms are inseparable from the connections formed between people, technology, and organizations.

Six important forces are in play at the Crossroads of an industry, company, or process:

1. **Code becomes more meaningful.** At the Crossroads, enriched Code Halos are now essential determinants to either winning or losing in the market. Disney, P&G, and Zappos all compete on their ability to manage data and information. Products become smarter and more efficient in how they give and receive data as their Code Halos become smarter with growth. The "Give-to-Get" equation makes sense for customers, and they understand

that algorithms are essential (if invisible) to their user experience. At the Crossroads, market success and failure is based on wisdom and insight derived from Code Halos.

2. **Halo-based expectations go mainstream.** Once customers and employees experience the value of Code Halos, the way they think about companies within their industry, and the industry itself, changes forever. They grumble now about a company that forces them to interact *without* some form of digital enhancement. They are ready to click away from companies that don't engage with them through their personal Code Halos. We can't go back. Our expectations of more efficient and flexible commerce and a more switched-on workplace have changed forever.

3. **Business processes "melt."** Data intensity—fueled by information from social, mobile, and cloud-enabled services—changes the nature of the organization. Connections among customers, ecosystem partners, products or devices, and employees are re-formed. At the Crossroads, old business processes melt under the heat of new insights and remold as digitized and digitally enabled constructs. For example, P&G once exclusively developed its products internally. However, the company realized this method cut it off from promising ideas that existed outside its offices. The company now employs external developers for products such as the Swiffer Duster and the Pulsonic Toothbrush. Sales is no longer about how to sell a product in person, but how to identify who might be interested in a product before he or she ever walk into your store—or arrive at your Web page—based on knowledge garnered through Code Halos.

4. **The algorithm links the chain.** The feelings of intimacy and familiarity we have when engaging with Code Halo-driven platforms such as Netflix, Pandora, Hulu, LinkedIn, Facebook, and the other digital winners come as a result of how well their algorithms "know" us. At the Crossroads, complex algorithms are inseparable from the connections formed between people, technology, and organizations.

5. **Software eats the process.** Marc Andreessen, co-creator of the first commercially successful Web browser, was right when he predicted that software would be at the center of industry disruption.[9] Applications and algorithms have become ever more critical to business decision-makers. We already see this in life sciences, banking, retail, and insurance—and software will become increasingly important in almost every industry.

6. **Value goes virtual.** These five preceding factors combine to shift the source of value—for customers, employees, partners, and investors—from hard assets to soft assets, from the physical to the virtual. At the Crossroads, investors are less focused on the value of hard assets—like factories, inventory, and retail outlets—and instead are focused on the value of virtual assets. This is what happened with the movie rental business and mobile phones.

Decide Your Fate at the Crossroads

The Crossroads Model—Ionization, Spark, Enrichment, and the Cross-roads—has played out in a dozen-plus major industries, and will play out in many others in the coming years. When Code Halos shift main-stream expectations of products, user experience, and ways of doing business, the transition from the old to the new is brutally efficient. In Chapter 7, "The Code Halo Economy: *The Economics of Information*," we highlight just how quickly value shifts in newly digitized markets.

CHAPTER SEVEN

The Code Halo Economy: The Economics of Information

If you've made it this far, you have a pretty good understanding of what Code Halos are and why they are likely to matter to your organization. Hopefully, you're excited and energized by the possibilities that Code Halos may bring to your organization. But by now your inner accountant is likely asking, "What's this going to cost? And what financial returns should I reasonably expect for my organization?"

To understand Code Halo economics in more detail, we collaborated with Oxford Economics and futurist Thornton May to survey 300 Global 2000 corporations as to their plans, methods, and expectations of generating value from the fields of information all around them.[1] We conducted dozens of interviews with leading companies in insurance, banking and financial services, healthcare, life sciences, technology, consumer goods/retail, manufacturing, and communications/media across the United States, the UK, Germany, and France.

We found that the business stakes of managing on information are exceptionally high (see Figure 7.1.) Among those who participated in our research, investment in business analytics yielded an average 8.4% increase in revenues and an average 8.1% improvement in cost reductions in the last financial year—**$766 billion in economic benefit over the past year alone.** If the surveyed companies deployed industry best practices, leaders estimate they could create an additional $853 billion of value. In short, from this research it is clear that competing on meaning and insight now stands as a potentially large value-creation lever for most organizations.

While these estimates may seem enormous, they are in line with the findings of other analysts. In 2011, McKinsey & Company found that the application of analytics in the U.S. healthcare system alone

The Value of Signal (and the Cost of Noise):
The New Economics of Meaning-Making

EVERY DAY WE CREATE **2.5** exabytes of data[1]

equivalent to 125,000 years' worth of DVD-quality video[2]

90%
of the world's data was created in the last two years[3]

Is data the new oil?

Organizations that can **separate signal from noise** are already winning in the market …

SMAC: a $360B market by 2016[4] ▼

$bn — 2016

200

100

20

Social Mobile Analytics Cloud

Over the past year
"Meaning Makers" benefit from:

▲ **11.3%**
Boost in revenue

▼ **10.7%**
Reduction in cost

DATA ABOUT DATA

$10.1T
Total 2011 revenue of the S&P 500.[5]

$766B
Economic impact from business analytics (revenues and savings) on surveyed firms over the past 12 months.

$57B
New value accessible if surveyed organizations used best "meaning making" practices.

1. IBM (http://ibm.co/1mKv8it) 2. *SearchStorage* (http://bit.ly/1dRxkSW)
3. *Science Daily* (http://bit.ly/JJazn7) 4. Cogizant analysis of industry reports
5. *Leader Capital News* (http://bit.ly/1mXr7Y4) All other data is from a 2013 Cogizant/Oxford Economics study.

Figure 7.1

could potentially unlock over $300 billion in new value annually, of which over two-thirds would be in the form of reductions to national healthcare expenditures.[2] In this light, the results of our own analysis may well be conservative.[3]

The data has to tell a story that matters to a real-life decision-maker. That narrative—and the business decisions it drives—is what "making meaning" is all about.

Meaning Makers Are Winning Based on Code

While the potential for value creation is vast, through our research it has become clear that not all companies leverage data and Code Halos in the same way. Our study defined respondents as one of three types: Meaning Makers, Data Collectors, and Explorers.

The Meaning Makers (26% of the survey panel) are the companies that have begun to master the ability to generate meaning and insight from their analysis of Big Data. They integrate business analytics in their daily work more effectively than others, are more effective at using analytic tools, create well-defined teams that focus on wringing value from data, and derive value in at least five of 10 key areas (ranging from basic financial reporting to sophisticated predictive modeling). These firms also believe they are ahead of their industry peers in using data analysis. The Data Collectors (24% of the panel) lag behind industry leaders in meaning-making activities. The Explorers (the remaining 50%) are in the middle of the pack. The differences in expectations for revenue growth across these three groups are striking:

- **Meaning Makers anticipate outsized revenue gains.** Over the next two years, 15% of Meaning Makers expect to see revenue growth of more than 10%—which is about three times more than average expectations.

- **Data Collectors are missing this shift point entirely—and are already paying for it.** Companies that lack capabilities in business analytics sense that this will negatively impact their growth prospects. Only about 18% of Data Collectors anticipate revenue growth of 5% or more over the next two years, compared with 39% of Meaning Makers.

- **Explorers expect good growth, but miss the potential upside.** Nearly half (49%) of Explorers and 42% of Data Collectors anticipate a relatively healthy 5% to 10% revenue growth rate over the next 24 months. But 15% of Meaning Makers anticipate sustained growth of greater than 10%, three times the rates of the others.

Steps to Make Meaning

Our research uncovered the steps executives need to take to apply the new economics of meaning-making in the near term. Every company is different, so there is no single "right" answer; but there are several clear mandates:

- **Just "doing analytics" is not enough.** The key to cracking the code is to *find the story* in the bits and bytes, and come away with tangible, **actionable** business meaning. The data has to tell a story that matters to a real-life decision-maker. That narrative—and the business decisions it drives—is what "making meaning" is all about.

- **Reimagine work at the process level, through analytics.** Organizations should focus on any business process that shapes at least 20% of costs or revenues—such as the underwriting process, clinical drug trials, wealth management services, supply chains, or customer relationship management. To seize competitive advantage, look at the data that you are—and could be—exchanging and using for value there.

- **Build a business analytics ecosystem.** Data is being created far more quickly than we are developing analytical talent sophisticated enough to make sense of it all—so there will not be enough supply to keep up with demand. Hiring and training will be parts of the solution, as will tools; but savvy decision-makers know that building an ecosystem of consultants and service providers is crucial for bringing the right capabilities to the organization.

Getting Analytics Right

The term analytics has come to sound almost mysterious, as if it is an arcane practice of robe-wearing Druids working from some secret, unknowable location deep within the labyrinth of the organization.

It is not that. Thomas Davenport—President's Distinguished Professor in Management and Information Technology at Babson College, author, and one of the leading thinkers in business and technology—defines the term as "all of the tools, techniques, goals, analysis processes, and business strategies used to transform data into actionable insights for business problem-solving and competitive advantage."[4] Using human judgment to decide what the data means is an essential element of the business analytics process.

Separating Signal from Noise Will Be the Killer Business Skill over the Next Decade

Companies have long employed some form of sales analytics; the difference today is the role of the SMAC Stack technologies.[5] "Big Data has been with us forever," comments Randy Krotowski, vice president in the Global Information Services Division of Caterpillar Inc. "The big change is that we are now [implementing] more things, so we are getting data from more stuff"—whether from a cell tower, a package, an assembly line, or a credit card reader.[6]

True analytics leaders have decided that meaning-making isn't just a part of their strategy—it *is* the strategy. Or as Jack Levis, United Parcel Service's director of process management, puts it: "We used to be a trucking company with technology. Now we are a technology company with trucks."

UPS May Like Logistics, But It Loves Data Even More

UPS has improved its business by applying analytics to sort package loads, order and route delivery runs, and measure the efficiency of each delivery truck's engine—with stunning results. It's helped the company eliminate some 85 million miles per year from drivers' routes, and reduce fuel consumption by some 8 million gallons. By analyzing historical data, UPS data scientists can excavate counterintuitive patterns, predict future probabilities and trends, and determine new ways to conduct business and prescribe better outcomes.

As Levis explains, "You want to be able to make predictions and ask, 'Where am I headed?' Moving from data to information to knowledge is what is going on in the world around us."

UPS documents everything it does. Drivers receive a 73-page manual detailing almost every process—how best to start their engines, which routes to follow, and even which pocket they should use for pen storage. This may sound like a modernized form of Taylorism, but UPS employees take pride in being rigorous—and the company rewards its drivers for best-in-class service.[7]

An excellent example of SMAC Stack innovation is the UPS DIAD tablet (introduced in 1991 but frequently updated). Drivers use these tablets to make real-time decisions about how to deliver most efficiently in order to save time, cut costs, improve productivity, and raise customer service levels. UPS drivers also carried GPS devices long before they were commonplace. The company monitors and measures every drop-off. "We track where every package is, every moment of the day," Levis says. For UPS, shaving one mile per driver per day is worth $50 million in savings annually. And one minute saved per driver per day prevents $14 million in unnecessary expense.

UPS has even made its package labels smart by having them specify which shelf on each truck drivers should load each parcel onto. They also inform the driver when a recipient is expecting delivery. The goal is to make it easy for any driver to turn around in his vehicle and immediately locate the next parcel to off-load. *"Little chunks of time cost a lot,"* Levis says.

Business Analytics Drives Both Cost Containment and Revenue Growth

Our research also found differences in the way organizations in different industries are competing on code.

- **Banking, financial services, and insurance companies generate the most value.** Decision-makers in banking are already clearly recognizing the value potential from business analytics. Companies in this sector indicate that 10% of revenue and 10.1% of costs are directly affected by how well they make meaning from the business information available to them. The insurance sector is close behind in terms of total economic impact resulting from business analytics.

- **Heavy machines don't inhibit competing on meaning.** Though it might seem counterintuitive to some, manufacturing companies generate a significant level of value by employing business analytics. These organizations use business analytics to grow revenue by improving sales, informing new product and service development, and carrying out financial planning and reporting. Quite logically, manufacturing companies achieve significant cost savings by making meaning around their manufacturing processes.

- **Consumer goods and retail lag other sectors.** With only 6.6% of revenue and 6% of costs affected by business analytics, the retail and consumer goods space seems to offer a particularly large opportunity to create value. It's clear that leaders in this sector should take meaningful steps to catch up to other industries.

- **Life Sciences and Communications, Information, Media, and Entertainment (CIME) are out of balance.** Most industry sectors in our study seem to have a reasonable handle on making meaning to drive both revenue and cost savings. Life sciences and CIME show the biggest variance. CIME in particular has almost a 1.3% variance between revenue and cost savings benefits—several times the difference in other sectors. It's likely that both industry sectors have an opportunity to balance their use of business analytics to drive economic impact.

There are tight connections between business analytics, revenue growth, and cost savings. Last year, Meaning Makers boosted profits by a full 9.9% more than Data Collectors. If the laggards merely caught up to the Meaning Makers, their overall productivity would improve immensely. In addition, more than 25% of respondents said that managing on meaning impacted revenue growth most when it was embedded into the processes at the customer interfaces—sales, marketing, and customer service. More than 26% pointed out that their companies are growing because they use business analytics to shape new product and service development. Perhaps most importantly, there is a huge performance chasm between Meaning Makers and Data Collectors. On average, Meaning Makers have a 23% advantage on cost savings and a 28% revenue advantage.

Build a Business Analytics Ecosystem

Managing on meaning can also help companies look forward and become more predictive. The change of the focus from the rear-view mirror (studying data from the past) to looking through the windshield (using data to predict future patterns) can help leaders drive the company to new levels. Anticipating customers, world events, weather patterns, supply chains, and other factors' future behaviors allows companies to deploy resources more effectively, reduce downtime, and adjust staff levels to match customer demand.

We expect the use of predictive modeling to grow 49% over the next 24 months (see Figure 7.2). We will see this change especially in the insurance and banking sectors, areas that find these tools especially helpful in developing new products and pricing options.

Surge Expected in Predictive Analytics

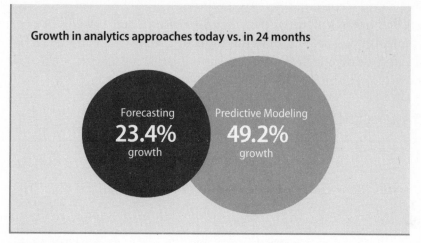

Growth in analytics approaches today vs. in 24 months

Forecasting
23.4%
growth

Predictive Modeling
49.2%
growth

Response base: 300
Prepared for Cognizant by Oxford Economics, October 2013

Figure 7.2

Skills for "Key-Making" Will Be Needed—But Are in Short Supply

As companies compete on Code Halos, make their operations more nimble, and gain more value from their use of SMAC Stack technologies, they find they need a different and expanded skill set in the workforce. Respondents in our survey believe that success will largely depend on having the right talent.

- Sixty-five percent of respondents already use technology experts who can help companies bridge gaps in IT and establish the right infrastructure to use analytics more effectively.
- Sixty percent employ software developers who design and apply analytical software that boosts efficiency and effectiveness.

In addition to technology experts and software developers, leading companies are looking for people with different kinds of experience and expertise and who can bring a different perspective to the proceedings. As a result, they are making hires that even five years ago might have seemed anomalous, even odd. Nearly 81% of respondents indicate that in the future the biggest growth in demand will be not for technical expertise, but for **behavioral scientists** who conduct research into and draw conclusions about how people are likely to act in the future (see Figure 7.3).

Behavioral Scientists Decode "What Happens Next"

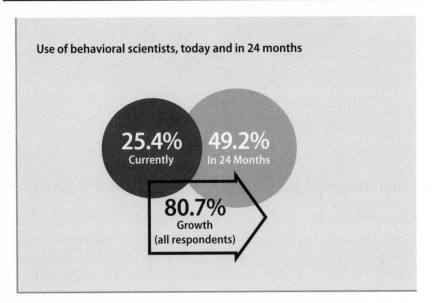

Response base: 300
Prepared for Cognizant by Oxford Economics, October 2013

Figure 7.3

Contributions from behavioral scientists will be instrumental in a company's efforts to develop more powerful tools to understand "how customers acted" in relation to company products and services, and also to predict "how customers will react next" to new developments. More than 31% of respondents say that demand will also be high for analytics subject-matter experts who can convert the business challenges and key questions into analytical approaches that can be executed by statisticians.

As Big Data explodes into "Colossal Data," the need for experts to work with it will explode as well, and there will not be enough expertise to go around. It won't be easy to find and attract the needed talent—especially for companies that don't have a reputation as market-leading meaning makers. While many are confident they can win the "war for talent" among analytics specialists, many will be left behind. Another survey that Oxford Economics recently conducted indicates that companies will face severe shortages in finding the Big Data talent they will need.[8]

Yet not all companies seem to anticipate the likely crunch. Some 26% of respondents intend to *reduce* their reliance on external partners to help with their needs for business analytics, and 19% have no plans at all to engage in external partnerships. Either these companies are especially good at recruiting Big Data experts, or they are underestimating the competition they will inevitably face.

At Toyota, a New Data Dashboard Solves a Problem and Delivers New Insights

In 2010, Toyota Motor faced a sudden crisis. Reports of unintended acceleration in some of its cars forced Toyota to issue two separate safety recalls covering millions of vehicles, and suspend sales of eight of its best-selling vehicles. The move cost the company and its dealers millions of dollars in lost sales revenue. As a result of the intense media coverage and speculation, the number of inquiries to the Toyota call center rose from 3,000 a day to 96,000. Warranty claims soared five-fold, overwhelming Toyota's infrastructure.

Toyota executives realized to their horror that despite the enormous volume of inquiries coming into their call center and warranty lines, and even with the vast amount of data they had accumulated, they still could not get a handle on how widespread the problem might be.

"The challenge was to disprove a negative" by conclusively demonstrating the vehicles were indeed safe, said Zack Hicks, CIO of Toyota

Motor Sales. "How do you do that? We have the data. We should be able to do something with that. The problem is that the data is unstructured. When does this become information?"

Hicks and his team took action. They built a "safety dashboard" to merge data from the National Highway Traffic Safety Administration (NHTSA) with Toyota's customer and parts databases, data from the call centers, vehicle buybacks, and other sources. This gave executives deeper insights into how well the cars performed and whether any patterns existed in reported safety complaints.

"It was incredible. It was like adding navigation onto a car," Hicks says. The safety dashboard delivered lots of insights. The team could see whether more complaints came from one region of the nation than another, or from areas where there had been extensive news coverage of the acceleration problem. The dashboard gave Toyota a far better understanding of the problem, and eventually helped it win exoneration from the NHTSA and the National Aeronautics and Space Administration, which found that neither software flaws nor mechanical problems caused unintended acceleration accidents.[9]

Now engineers and finance executives inside Toyota use the dashboard to better understand how cars are performing, and anticipate problems before they arise. People within Toyota who were accustomed to looking at only narrow slices of data from within their own divisions "now essentially can do a regression analysis against different types of data to see if there are new meanings, new relationships," Hicks said. "That is power. That is the opportunity."

"Return on Insight" Is the New ROI

Dramatically improved performance no doubt sounds great. Our study results show the scale of opportunity to help your organization based on new ways of leveraging Code Halos and business analytics. However, we have to recognize the rules of the game inside virtually any organization. These solutions are new, innovative, and require an entrepreneurial mindset to bring them to life (more on that later, in Chapter 10).

There are plenty of sources that describe how to construct a solid return on investment (ROI) and business case, so we're not going to go into that here. Instead, we'll cover the Code Halo-specific considerations. Regardless of an organization's size, most business decisions these days require at least a rough indication of ROI. If you have an innovative idea, you'll have to sell the economics. We've provided some rules to help structure your ideas in Part II, so you may need to return here after you've been through that section of the book. Of course, each business should be reviewed based on its own merit, but there are some general tactics for success.

Pick the Right Target for Disruption

Based on our market observations, organizations are creating Code Halo solutions at one of four levels—each of which has a different cost/benefit equation.

Applying Code Halos to long-accepted practices can unlock value from a process that had seemed carved into stone.

- **Industrial market disrupters:** These are the real game changers for a traditional company or an industry built on an industrial physical supply chain. You don't need to bet a billion dollars to change a market; but if you are in a large enterprise and intend to alter air travel, or insurance, or auto manufacturing completely, you may need to make a significant investment.
- **Digital market disrupters:** Nobody knew they needed to watch videos at home until Blockbuster and thousands of small video shops tapped into a latent mass market. Then Netflix came along and moved the entire process to a virtual transaction that preceded shipping physical discs and tapes. Now, of course, Netflix has pioneered an entirely new business model. Netflix's investments started small—let's send tapes through the

mail—with an amount less than $3 million.[10] The Huffington Post started with only $2 million of seed capital.[11] Many online businesses fall into this category. They often begin as eBusiness ideas that blossom to disrupt a market sector.

- **Process disrupters:** Some innovators look at a work process and think, "That's ridiculous." Applying Code Halos to long-accepted practices—claims processing, underwriting, application management and procurement—can unlock value from a process that had seemed carved into stone. That's what happened to waiting in line to withdraw cash from a bank teller. Banking itself was not reinvented, but many personal cash management processes were disrupted. Investments here can be relatively modest, depending on the scope and scale of the change.

- **Process improvers:** For many smaller companies or divisions, merely improving a process—usually around the customer interface—is a great way to explore Code Halos. These investments often use social media, cloud-based tools, and personal mobile devices to make costs very low. For a café or taxi company, Square Wallet does not change the fact that money is changing hands, but it dramatically improves the payment process.

Every solution will be different, and there are so many variables that no single formula will give you a perfect answer. How much should it cost? How much revenue will you generate? It would be great to know these beforehand, but the plain truth is that Code Halo solutions are innovations, and inherently risky. The trick is to make informed choices so you can fail fast and learn. Part III, "Winning with the Crossroads Model," has more detailed ideas and guidance on how to develop your ROI.

Making Meaningful Returns

By now, you know that competing based on meaning and insight will be the biggest value lever in your business. The question is—how will you pull that lever?

Companies that are able to make meaning from business analytics are already winning. They're reaping significant rewards from running better, improving process efficiency, and operating differently by using insight to reimagine work. Decision-makers already expect that investments here will pay off in the near term. The power of insight is beginning to shape markets and disrupt business processes.

The companies that ultimately win and decode the new economics of meaning-making will be the ones that reimagine work, see business processes and customers as sources of insight, and find ways to keep human judgment and values embedded into real-world business decisions. We're well beyond theory building by now, and these trends will only accelerate in the coming quarters and years.

Summary of Part I

Digits Over Widgets: The Next Age of Business and Technology

We've seen in Part I how a handful of companies have created a trillion dollars of value based on Code Halos. We looked at how SMAC Stack technologies are the new foundation of Code Halos, and examined how organizations are using Code Halos to connect employees, products, and customers. We also dissected the anatomy of a winning Code Halo solution and described the downside of missing any of the essential components. We looked at market data to illustrate the powerful and predictable pattern for disruption that we call the Crossroads Model, and we presented a data-intensive look at the economics of information to show just how big this shift will be for organizations large and small, public and private.

People and organizations are still creating a map for the way forward. However, we already know a lot about what works and what does not. There are some critical rules you can follow to significantly increase your chances of success. In Part II, we'll focus on "Four Principles for Success in the Code Halo Economy."

PART II

FOUR PRINCIPLES FOR SUCCESS IN THE CODE HALO ECONOMY

CHAPTER EIGHT

Delivering Beautiful Products and Experiences

"We are in an era where we are reimagining nearly everything … powered by new devices, plus connectivity, plus new user interfaces, plus beauty."

—MARY MEEKER, PARTNER, KLEINER, PERKINS, CAUFIELD & BYERS, NOVEMBER 2012[1]

Beauty is probably not the first word that springs to mind when you think about most corporate computer systems. Yet consumer-based Code Halo products and experiences have raised the bar by making beauty a priority. We're reading headlines like these more frequently:

- "Apple iPhone 4: an object of **rare beauty** that leapfrogs the competition."[2]
- "FuelBand is a stunner.… FuelBand is such an **elegant, beautiful product** that some users might consider buying it solely for the watch functionality."[3]
- "Netflix—**beautiful, beautiful Netflix**—is, experts hypothesize, the pinnacle of the human experience."[4]

Do your customers, partners, and employees look at your company's IT systems and gush with such sentiments?

We humans are inherently drawn to great design. Multiple studies have shown that the human eye is captivated by the visually pleasing—and, what's more, that the hand instinctively wants to *touch* beautiful objects.

Many IT departments have not developed this design sensibility—but they must, and quickly. Design will be a critical factor of success for IT organizations over the next five years. For the past several decades, most corporate IT systems have been developed for captive IT users—primarily employees—who were *forced* to use them. Most Code Halos, on the other hand, are elective systems, whose users can choose to opt in—or out. As such, beauty of design has become mandatory. For a Code Halo to become a truly compelling part of one's life, it must elicit a visceral appeal.

"Beauty," under our definition, does not simply cover the physical aspects of a Code Halo, of how its amplifier and application interface appear. This quality needs to transcend the physical to the entire customer experience and business model. For example, a Waze GPS might have a fun and funky appearance on your smartphone, but the app's true attractiveness is in its ability to enhance one's driving experience. It ensures the fastest route around traffic, notifies users of accidents, road hazards, and speed traps, and creates a sense of community on the road.

This chapter will explore the three main actions leadership teams can take to make Code Halos fundamentally attractive and compelling:

- **Action #1: Make it physically beautiful.** A Code Halo battle can be won or lost over this single issue—our desire to have, and use, beautiful things. So how do you go about building beautiful amplifiers and application interfaces, and the supporting organization to do this on a continual basis?

- **Action #2: Create moments of magic—through correlations found in Big Data.** How do you dazzle customers with those "Aha!" moments of deep personal connection? While it may feel like magic to the Code Halo user ("How did they know that was my favorite song in high school?"), it is the science of analytics at work. In continually recognizing and implementing against the correlations found in Code Halo databases, we can generate moments of highly customized engagement, driving deeper loyalty to your Code Halo solution.

- **Action #3: Make it virtually beautiful.** Beauty is more than skin deep. Companies generate a successful Code Halo business model with new levels of scale and scope when management focuses more on the virtual—the data, analytics, and the overall business ecosystem—than on the physical. How does one lead this change management exercise?

Let's look at each of these actions in more detail.

Action #1: Make It Physically Beautiful

The success of many Code Halo pioneers had much to do with compelling design—to lead customers to an irrational sense of connection and loyalty. Yet as the truism goes, beauty is in the eye of the beholder. Any number of things can be beautiful—a supermodel on a magazine cover, a Bugatti, a Renaissance painting, a gymnast's leap, or a platter of sushi. And of course, one who appreciates the beauty of the Bugatti may not appreciate gymnastics, and vice versa.

Similarly, the beauty of Google, the Apple iPhone, and Microsoft Xbox have been instrumental to the success of those Code Halo pioneers. Yet each case conveys a different form of beauty, designed for different people and purposes. So, before we explore these varying forms—and determine which is best for a particular initiative—it's best to address some universal truths, three fundamentals of aesthetics, to which your solution must adhere:

1. **Visually stunning:** Does your Code Halo—through both its amplifier and interface—truly "pop" visually? Does it elicit the psychological response (e.g., relief, comfort, or excitement) that you want from its user? How do its colors, shapes, and structure draw you in? Does it bring new life and attraction to an old product category?

2. **Elegant:** Is it graceful and stylish? Does it bring a form of art to something previously considered a utility? Is it capable of

becoming something of a fashion statement?

3. **Simple and intuitive:** Can one learn how to use your halo in a matter of minutes? Does it fit within—and even catalyze or enhance—your work or personal routine? Or, conversely, is it so complex that it is intimidating?

We first cited the example of the Nest thermostat in Chapter 3, a tool that hits all three of these criteria. It brings a sense of design, elegance, and beauty to that strange and ugly device found in every home, the thermostat. Not only is the physical amplifier newly beautiful, but so is the application interface (on any mobile device or computer), as well as the overall experience of managing the temperature in one's home—anywhere, at any time. Nest has redefined something elemental, and has captured market attention by doing it with style.

Engineering and Design Must Connect to Create Beautiful Code Halo Solutions

We can no longer ignore the beauty of design and the design of beauty. Both must become institutionalized within your organization. Yet great design in the majority of today's corporate technology departments would best be described as a "growth area." While most IT organizations are deeply proficient in "left brain" analytical activities, they are typically lacking in "right brain" creative pursuits.

Nurturing and developing these creative capabilities is not a trivial activity. It quite often requires a jump-start in launching serious design capabilities—most often by hiring a strong third-party design firm or internal senior designers. But this jump-start is only a beginning. Management must create a supportive culture for these new folks, who will likely feel like strangers in a strange land at first. They will dress differently, have different work styles, and—most important—initially have differing definitions of success. It will feel as if your traditional IT staff is a group of Mr. Spocks—highly rational, analytical, and risk-averse—while the new designers are more like Captain Kirk—brash, emotional, and risk-taking. As one of our clients put it, "the IT leader of the future will look like the love-child of Spock and Kirk." In other words, it will be someone who can deliver solutions with a combination of right-brain and left-brain thinking and implementation.

To showcase the importance of beauty—and the necessity to combine engineering with design within the organization—let's look at an industry that's been integrating design and technology for decades and therefore has a lot of lessons for IT and business leaders. We'll explore the case of Jaguar Cars and the Lincoln Motor Company (a division of the Ford Motor Company).

While now independent from one another, the British automaker Jaguar was part of the Ford Motor Company from 1990 to 2008. The vision of the relationship was not for Ford simply to own Jaguar as a stand-alone entity, but for the two manufacturers to leverage multiple synergies in designing and manufacturing luxury vehicles. As part of Ford's premier automotive group, Jaguar would share in Ford's R&D capabilities, design sensibilities, and production platforms.

During the latter days of this corporate marriage, design teams from both brands were tasked with creating the next-generation flagship car for each brand. Each vehicle was to be the centerpiece of the respective car lineups, be sold for between $40,000 and $60,000, and compete directly with the well-established and highly-respected BMW 5 Series and Mercedes Benz E-Class Series. By 2005, both Lincoln and Jaguar, for differing reasons, had badly tarnished reputations in their market segments; customers often viewed them as being inferior to established competitors. Even worse, relative upstarts such as Audi and Lexus were producing vehicles that were seen as superior to those of the venerable brands, and Cadillac was in the midst of a design-led resurgence.

The pressure was on Ford's and Jaguar's designers. These two groups—operating within the same corporate entity—were given roughly the same assignment, at the same time, with generally the same resources and under very similar constraints and market pressures. They had access to all the same technical inputs, including market research, competitive analyses, design techniques and tools, technical advances, and more. The two designs they produced, however, were wildly different—and generated divergent business results.

The designers at Lincoln unveiled the Lincoln MKS, which elicited a massive yawn from the market.

It was widely viewed as a Ford Taurus with leather seats, and confirmed the impression that Lincoln was run by accountants and not to be taken seriously as a luxury carmaker.[5] At a time when Lincoln badly needed to revitalize its brand—by launching a beautiful car at the heart of its line—the MKS failed to deliver.

Jaguar designers, on the other hand, produced the gorgeous and now world-acclaimed XF which, by any definition, has again made Jaguar highly relevant.[6]

Critics were effusive in their praise when the XF was unveiled:

> "With the XF, Jaguar has created a completely original design …"[7]

> "When the concept-car predecessor of the Jaguar XF was introduced at the 2007 Detroit Auto Show, many in the audience actually stood and applauded its sleek design."[8]

> "Great Jaguars are design showcases," Ian Callum, the brand's Design Director, said with emotion. "That's our mantle, and we're taking it back."[9]

Source: Jaguar XF Image © Jaguar Land Rover Ltd. Used with permission.

In other words, Jaguar was serious about creating a culture that attracted and motivated great designers—and allowed them not to just cohabitate with, but thrive among, strong engineering talent. Years later, Jaguar's XF continues to sweep up industry recognition and awards, including *Auto Express* magazine's "Car of the Decade" award.

What's important—and what may have driven the management team at Lincoln to distraction—is that the two cars are quite similar from a purely technical standpoint. You would be hard-pressed to find meaningful differences in terms of on-road performance, quality of production, and customer amenities. Yet one car failed to revitalize a brand. The difference? Design.

As a postscript to this case study, it seems that Lincoln learned its lesson, as its 2013 version of the MKS, and the lower-end 2013 MKZ sedan, have come to market with significantly improved designs. In fact, by 2013, the MKS had become an award-winner (e.g., it won the best overall value award from Intellichoice in 2013).

Why is this case study so instructive and why is it germane to Code Halos? One key reason: it highlights the importance of the amplifier's design and beauty. Far too many corporate IT departments think the same way the Lincoln MKS design team did: that is, focus on delivering technical proficiency, employing a classic IT "build it and they will come" mentality. This approach will not suffice in the coming Code Halo battles. The team at Jaguar understood this and thought like the Code Halo veterans, with a perspective of, "Being technically solid is table stakes. My product must also have a visual, visceral appeal."

We have seen this failure time and time again in our consulting travels, as many corporate IT organizations are currently out of their depth when it comes to generating beauty. As one manager put it, "It's like a bunch of morticians trying to throw a wedding." Thus, attract design proficiency to your organization—either by hiring or via partnerships and, in some cases, acquisition—and create a culture to allow it to flourish.

Beauty Is About Experience, Not Just Devices

While the Jaguar XF versus Lincoln MKS example demonstrates the importance of amplifier beauty, that's only half the battle with Code Halos. A beautiful consumer experience is also central to success, and in many cases is more difficult to achieve—since it often requires us to rethink business processes and organizational models, along with the heavy lifting of change management. This can be particularly difficult for an established organization, since it needs to accomplish it in parallel—and often in conflict—with existing business models and channels.

Why the Nook Found No Niche

Consider Barnes & Noble's failed tablet, the Nook, which suffered a fate similar to the Zune (as discussed in Chapter 3). The misstep was due to an excessive focus on the amplifier—which was, by the way, a beautiful physical machine—with limited thought given to the application and overall *experience.* As a result, Barnes & Noble suffered substantial financial and reputational loss.

The Nook *should have* succeeded. Barnes & Noble has a strong brand and loyal customers; the book industry is unambiguously going digital; and tablet sales have been booming. In 2012, they grew 78% worldwide with 128 million units sold; growth rates were predicted to more than double through 2017.[10] In October of 2012—just two years after introducing the iPad—Apple shipped its one hundred millionth tablet. Amazon's Kindle sales doubled from 2011 to 2012, and accounted for roughly one in five tablet sales in the United States.[11] Yet the Nook's sales were *declining* through 2012,[12] and Barnes & Noble halted production of the machine by the middle of 2013.

How did Barnes & Noble so badly miss this party? The market seemed ready-made for them, and was one in which there was already great evidence of success. Unlike Borders—which completely missed the eBusiness transition—Barnes & Noble seemed to have jumped on the bandwagon just in time.

They had the right idea. But they had the wrong implementation.

In short, the Nook didn't generate a beautiful experience. It failed to produce the necessary *"Wow, how did they read my mind?"* effect. In other words, the process of discovery that a Barnes & Noble customer may have when walking the aisles of its retail stores was not an experience that the Nook replicated. By failing to meet—if not exceed—the beauty of the physical Barnes & Noble experience, the Nook experience violated the Barnes & Noble brand promise. And what was even worse—it paled badly in comparison to its competitors, Apple and Amazon, both masters of Code Halo thinking.

The focus of the Nook team on the hardware device—at the expense of the algorithms and overall business model—was particularly devastating as the amplifier was quickly commoditizing, and those customers who were purchasing either an iPad or Android-based tablet were not going to *also* buy a Nook. For Barnes & Noble to attempt to win in digital markets by producing its own amplifier is akin to Arista Records or RKO Records, in the 1970s, trying to build a market by manufacturing their own record players.

Code Halo beauty must transcend the amplifier, through the application and the experience generated by Big Data and algorithms.

So why did Amazon build the Kindle, and how was it successful? Simple. Amazon had all of the elements in place to make the Kindle experience a beautiful one. Amazon already had a successful application interface through Amazon.com. It had highly sophisticated algorithms created from mountains of data it had been collecting and analyzing for years. Amazon also had an incredibly robust business ecosystem on the back end—allowing it not to simply fulfill the reading needs of its customers, but many associated needs as well. Amazon, in other words, already had the **full anatomy** of a Code Halo: interface, amplifier, Big Data, algorithms, and business model. Delivering its experience through a different amplifier—the Kindle as opposed to a PC—was a seamless transition and provided a similarly beautiful overall experience.

The Nook initiative, on the other hand, failed because of poor management of Code Halos and the lack of a sophisticated anatomy.

This failure to understand and thus compete in the Code Halo economy has had a devastating effect on Barnes & Noble. The firm is at a strategic crossroads. Will it try again, or retreat and focus solely on being a traditional, physical-book retailer? This unanswered question is creating confusion. As market observer Mike Shatzkin, CEO of Idea Logical, has stated, "Barnes & Noble cannot ultimately escape the fate of Blockbuster and Virgin [Megastore]. But they have to make the slide into oblivion more gradual. Does Barnes & Noble have three years or 10 years? I don't know. But it doesn't have 20 years, that's for sure. They have to manage their disappearance or turn into something completely different."[13]

The bottom-line lesson of the Nook? Code Halo beauty must transcend the amplifier, through the application and the experience generated by Big Data and algorithms.

Action #2: Create Moments of Magic Through Correlations Found in Big Data

We know that on their own, Code Halos can generate significant insight into people, products, and processes. Those insights are quickly multiplied when Code Halos connect—and they become both more accurate and more actionable.

Take, for example, your musical tastes. Keeping them to yourself does nothing to increase your knowledge of other music you might enjoy. Talking about them with a friend does little more. Only when your tastes, your Code Halo of interests, connects with the institutional Code Halo of a Pandora, Amazon, or Apple, does the value of Code Halos become readily apparent.

You might be surprised how much information these Code Halo intersections can provide (or predict) about a person based on very little data, such as just a few favorite musical artists or a handful of favorite songs. Recent studies have shown that musical tastes correlate with personality profiles, and that varying profiles correlate with how individuals wish to interact with retailers, what marketing approaches and messages resonate with them, and what and how they buy. According to The Echo Nest, a "music intelligence start-up," your music-based Code Halos can tell much more about you than just what kind of music you like to listen to.[14] They can also reveal your tastes in food, movies, and literature as well as your product preferences, political leanings, and even measures of intelligence. For example:

- **Movie tastes:** If you listen to Jimi Hendrix, you are likely to enjoy sci-fi movies. If you are a big fan of certain country music singers, odds are you will be annoyed by the Academy Awards because you do not agree with their selections, whereas "grunge" music fans usually greatly enjoy Academy Award-nominated films. And if you are a Justin Timberlake fan, there is a high probability you also enjoy Pixar films.[15]

- **Politics:** If you download a lot of Kenny Chesney and George Strait, it's likely you vote Republican. Listening to a lot of Madonna, Jay-Z, and Rihanna? You are going to vote for Democratic candidates the vast majority of the time. But if you're listening to the Beatles, the Rolling Stones, or Johnny Cash, you vote as a political centrist, going left or right with consistency.[16]

- **Personality profile:** Retailers have long understood that customers with differing personality profiles shop differently and make dissimilar kinds of purchases. For example, those who prefer "reflexive and complex" music—such as classical or jazz—are usually more open-minded and place a higher value on verbal communications. These buyers will listen to a well-articulated, rational value proposition. On the other hand, those who prefer "upbeat and conventional" music—such as pop, rock, and R&B—are more "feelers" who like extroversion (and rank lower in openness and verbal capability), and may be more swayed by louder, simpler, more emotionally based messages.[17]

Another important point is the finding that these music-based assessments of personality profiles have proven to be more accurate than assessments made face-to-face. You want to know how a buyer buys? Don't look at her clothing, hairstyle, or overall appearance; find out what she listens to.

By repeating this process of bringing different kinds of information together, Code Halo leaders are able to create engaging personalized experiences.

There are also strong correlations between musical tastes, IQ, recreational drug use, relationship status, sexual promiscuity, and even the family construct in which one grew up.[18] Also, musical preferences are a strong indicator of one's age. The majority of people "lock in" their musical preferences, as well as their favorite artists, between the ages of 17 and 24.

Thus, it's clear that knowing a customer's musical taste truly matters in retail markets. It's why today's consumer eBusiness leaders track this particular set of preferences so closely—either directly, or with partners such as Pandora.[19] Many of these platforms tailor their overall experience with you based largely on your musical preferences. Then, by considering your Code Halo's music data with other data—say, your literature preferences—the picture of who you are as a person becomes more finely pixilated. By repeating this process of bringing different kinds of information together, Code Halo leaders are able to create engaging personalized experiences.

While we have focused on musical tastes within consumer-based Code Halos—primarily because (a) most of us have experienced this phenomenon personally, and (b) the research is now rather robust in this field, such powerful correlations exist within *all* forms of Code Halos. Gone are the days where your marketing department would primarily utilize market research, demographics, and focus groups to craft customer value propositions and go-to-market strategies. Such broad-scale educated guessing will be replaced with individualized empiricism that is enabled by continually recognizing the correlations within your Code Halos—and thus driving experience beauty.

Action #3: Make It Virtually Beautiful

Beauty with Code Halos, as in the rest of life, is more than skin deep. These beautiful experiences have their foundation in business models that are designed to manage the virtual. Though a growing number of organizations are migrating the customer experience from the physical to the virtual, most are not *actively reshaping* their organizations to win by competing on information and knowledge processes—many of which are still rooted in traditional industrial-world thinking.

In implementing such knowledge processes across your organization, look to adhere to the five virtual effects now entering nearly every organization:

1. **The Google Effect: the separation of humans and information.** The last time you Googled something, did you stop and say, "Hmmm, I wonder if these results came from a database in a server farm in Oregon, Georgia, or Virginia, or maybe from the Netherlands or Australia?"[20] Of course not. Through the Google Effect, information and physical location in our personal lives have been fully virtualized and dematerialized. So why, in many corporations, are the two (very expensively) still colocated?

2. **The Skype Effect: free communications, death of distance.** There was a time when the physical distance between people on opposite ends of a phone line made a significant difference in the price of the call and the nature of the communication. In those days, overseas telecommunication was a true luxury. Today, IP-based communication platforms (whether video, voice, or email) have cost and usage bases entirely unrelated to physical distance. Speaking to someone on the other side of

the world through an IP network is no different from talking to them as if they lived across the street. Now that a global company can communicate with its customers and suppliers at a cost of next to nothing, a surfeit of information that used to be unaffordable to transmit is now affordable to consume.

3. **The Facebook Effect: the virtualization of human relationships.** Fundamental to Facebook's immense popularity is that it allows us to maintain personal relationships without requiring physical interactions. The same is now true in the corporate operating model, where working relationships based on capability and trust no longer require physical proximity.

4. **The LinkedIn Effect: the virtualization of specialized knowledge.** As mentioned in Chapter 3, LinkedIn allows us to map our professional networks and to quickly locate trusted expertise. Why can't all organizations work in the same manner? The LinkedIn Effect gives us a map of our professional networks. If companies leverage this kind of networking, it will enable the virtualization of expertise and allow an optimized degree of task-performance specialization.

5. **The Amazon Effect: the virtualization of customer experience.** Amazon knows you better than the manager at your corner store. In some ways, Amazon may even know you better than some of your family members. And yet, when was the last time you *met* anybody from Amazon? This virtualization of customer intimacy is led by, but is not the sole domain of the Trillion-Dollar Club. But it is available to all organizations and, in the next decade (driven by social CRM), will produce a massive dematerialization at the level of the user interface.

Beauty Is Becoming Central to Creating Value

Many business leaders will be uncomfortable with thinking about the notion of creating beauty, but it would be a mistake to overlook this or think of it as too soft or irrelevant. As outlined in this chapter—and our cautionary case illustrations—delivering beauty that transcends all aspects of your Code Halo solution is central to success. Beauty must go beyond just the physical to the full experience of the Code Halo. As stated by Johann Wolfgang von Goethe, "Beauty is everywhere a welcome guest."[21] Ensure your Code Halos are always welcome guests. Make them beautiful, inside and out.

In the next chapter we'll explore and provide guidance on how to manage the new complexities of privacy and ethics—and avoid evil— in a Code Halo world.

CHAPTER NINE

Don't Be Evil 2.0: Earning—and Keeping—Trust in a Transparent World

Despite the many benefits we've covered in previous chapters, we're only too aware that Code Halos have a potential dark side. These new models of commerce are ushering in questions on how organizations build and maintain trust, protect individuals' privacy, and conduct themselves ethically. We are living in a time when technology is moving faster than legal and cultural constructs, and this is creating significant confusion and even fear.

Many people experience a sense of trepidation when it comes to the growing virtual economy. We hear a lot of comments such as "Yes, but …

- … I don't want big businesses knowing all my personal information."
- … the government already knows too much about me."
- … this will be a hacker's paradise."
- … now I'll be bombarded by even more advertising and promotional junk."
- … how can I control my own information?"
- … this is the final nail in the coffin of privacy."
- … I am not a number."
- … I don't want to live in a 1984 world."

In the context of the 2013 National Security Agency (NSA) spying scandals, such Orwellian fears are valid and understandable—and we share many of them. *The Atlantic* magazine's Conor Friedersdorf put it well when he wrote about the NSA, "[We] are counting on having angels in office and making ourselves vulnerable to devils."[1]

We can't promise that nothing bad will happen when code meets code, and we can't ignore the dark side of the halo. Some of our fears are likely to materialize. People *will* get hacked. Government intrusion *will* grow. Marketers *will* create new ways to embed advertising into every nook and cranny of our lives through every IP-addressable form factor. Privacy *will* recede. Nefarious individuals *will* have new opportunities to harm us.

These challenges may slow but they won't stop the expansion of Code Halo solutions. Winning organizations need to recognize, understand, and actively manage these potential negative issues. To that end, this chapter has two sections: First, we aim to put these fears into a proper context by exploring a few key themes:

- We've experienced fears generated by new technologies before.
- The evolution of privacy.
- Trust is the currency of the Code Halo economy.
- The law will never catch up to the pace of technical innovation.

In the second section, we highlight five actions your organization can take to build trust and avoid evil:

1. Give your Code Halo a **delete** button.
2. Act with **transparency**: Show me you know me.
3. Demonstrate **value**: Shine a light on your Give-to-Get equation.
4. **Calibrate** your approach to the global stage.
5. Hard-code organizational **self-control.**

Section I: Putting the Dark Side into Context—Four Perspectives

Perspective #1: We've Been Here Before—Fears Generated by New Technologies

What if big business developed an innovation that, despite massive appeal, would also be the number one killer of children in the country; soil the environment; be the source of significant international tensions—even wars; and usher in entirely new categories of crime? This innovation sounds like it would never get off the ground. Yet today, pretty much all of us use this innovation without even thinking about its negative consequences.

Of course, we're talking about the automobile. Over the past century, most of us have come to a point of equilibrium with cars, balancing the benefits with the inherent risks. For example, as awful as car-associated crime is, we have collectively accepted a certain level of carjackings, drive-by shootings, smuggling, drunk-driving accidents, road rage, and basic car theft as part of the downside of personal transportation. We don't live in fear of our cars, as we have learned how to manage the risks. Most of us maintain our cars properly and drive defensively. We instinctively make decisions on car-related crime. For example, we may leave a car unlocked when parked at a friend's house in a leafy suburb, yet lock it up tight—and under a streetlamp—when parking on a Manhattan side street. In short, most car owners take appropriate precautions to avoid the risks inherent in driving and car ownership.

We do the same when we go online. When the *information highway* opened just a few years ago, we saw a wave of fear concerning privacy, control, intrusion, hacking, and depersonalization. Back then, we heard phrases like:

- "I'll never share my financial information on the computer."
- "I like buying books on Amazon, but there are things I will always want to buy at a store."

- "I can't believe the, um, stuff you can access on the Internet."
- "I will **never** let my kids go online."

Like the automobile, the commercialization of the Internet introduced new risks and forms of crime. Yet, that didn't stop the broad adoption of this innovation. Today there are 634 million websites and 2.4 billion Internet users.[2] And while a large percentage of users have concerns about privacy, hacking, loss of control, intrusion, piracy, and scamming, few swear off the Internet because of their concerns.

The point is that once we assimilate a new technology, we stop blaming the technology for its downside. However, we have yet to reach this level of assimilation with SMAC technologies. We still read headlines such as those concerning the "Craigslist Killer" highlighting the role of Craigslist in the murder of three farmhands in Ohio in 2011.[3] Of course, cars, guns, and phones were involved in the crimes as well—and arguably played much larger roles than social media—but the perpetrator wasn't characterized as the "Oldsmobile killer" or the "handgun killer" or the "AT&T killer." Such descriptions about fully assimilated technologies would sound absurd.

We see clearly how fear often stems simply from the "shock of the new." Fear of newfangled contraptions such as trains, automobiles, planes, and television spooked previous generations, but these are now well accepted in our society. This too will occur with Code Halos.

Perspective #2: The Evolution of Privacy

The borders of privacy are being redrawn, particularly along generational lines. This confuses individuals and companies about what is appropriate for us to share and reveal.

In the 1960s, the "Woodstock Generation" famously drew new societal boundaries around music, recreational drug use, sexuality, and fashion. Today, the Millennial Generation is ushering in change just as profound. However, because these changes are in the virtual and not the physical world, they are less obvious—and they come to a head with privacy.

We conduct so much of our lives online—shared, visible, transparent, open—and all proffered voluntarily by ourselves or our friends through Facebook, Twitter, Instagram, and Tumblr, or less voluntarily via our credit scores, phone records, and keystrokes that the government can impound without warrant. There's no denying that privacy is indeed receding.

Older generations look at their children's online postings—the party pics, sophomoric tweets, and constant relationship updates—as cringe-worthy. They see them as virtual time bombs that will inevitably explode at some point in the future in front of prospective employers, marriage prospects, and even lawyers or voters. Millennials, on the other hand, look at their parents' online conservatism with disdain and think, "If you're unwilling to be transparent, then you're uptight at best and dishonest at worst."

Elective versus Forced Revelations

While we collectively struggle to discern the lines of privacy, one issue has become clear: Privacy—or its removal—should be an *elective decision*. It should not be forced upon or away from anybody.

Location-based capabilities highlight the importance of user choice and opt-in. A prime example is comparing the Foursquare application to license plate readers in the United States. Foursquare is a software platform that, through your mobile device, will track and then communicate your every move to your chosen social networks. It has over 30 million customers who are more than willing to broadcast their daily movements. They are eager to provide this information, and forfeit a great deal of privacy, in order to enhance their social lives or allow them to find suitable restaurants, clubs, and stores in new neighborhoods.

At the same time, the government is proving quite capable of tracking individual citizens through the use of license plate readers.

Scanning cameras can be affixed to police cruisers, road signs, and tollbooths, and have proven effective in capturing enormous amounts of license plate data in the United States and elsewhere. The state of Maryland collected 85 million driver records in 2012, and each of the over 7 million registered vehicles in Los Angeles County were scanned 22 times on average.[4] In Minneapolis even the mayor's own car was scanned at 41 different locations.[5] And this is not just for states or larger municipalities. The local police department in Jersey City, New Jersey, which has a population of roughly 250,000, collected more than 2 million license plate images in 2012.[6]

Police departments argue that such scanning data is useful in solving and preventing crime. Maryland authorities stated that in the first five months of 2012, 29 million license plate scans enabled the police to track 132 wanted suspects.[7] Meanwhile, the backlash against these readers has surged; not just from the American Civil Liberties Union but also from an array of organizations and individual citizens. Many find mass scanning an example of government overreach and a violation of privacy and trust. Some people are incensed about not being informed that they are being constantly photographed and monitored as they drive around town.

This example highlights the importance of *elective* decisions regarding privacy, versus those that are forced or mandatory. The same consumer who freely elects to give out her precise movements on Foursquare may also feel enormously violated by the presence of license plate readers, because:

- Foursquare use is voluntary and controllable.
- The consumer trusts Foursquare as an organization, and her collection of Facebook friends who will see the data.
- The consumer values what she "gets"—an improved social life.

This same consumer, who may not trust the government, feels helpless as she cannot control this data on her car's Code Halo, and has no immediate "get" from such activities.

This is just one of many examples that bring attention to the privacy lines we are redrawing in our highly digitized world, and we expect numerous debates on privacy over the coming years. Later we'll show how you can resolve many such issues by ensuring that those in your Code Halo initiatives can manage their own privacy, instead of concluding that you have violated it.

Perspective #3: Trust Is the Currency of the Code Halo Economy

> *"It takes 20 years to build a reputation and five minutes to ruin it."*
>
> —Warren Buffett

Code Halos have become catalysts of trust, meaning they can both build and destroy it rapidly. Firms that have enhanced their brands with Code Halos have placed trust before near-term profits, and certainly before self-interest. Such firms have established a culture in which trust is viewed as the true currency of the Code Halo economy. When in doubt, they think, "What will best build trust with my customer?"

"Trust" can mean many things. Of course, it's about fundamental honesty, of being counted on to do the right thing. But it's also about quality; a customer *trusts* that your product will work. It's about punctuality, in being reliable for your customer. It's about consistency, in that your brand promise is fulfilled in all transactions, no matter how small. It's about openness and transparency in your dealings. And it's about fairness, that your pricing and business practices are reasonable.

There are many ways to represent the complexities of trust, but we've found the following equation to be useful:

$$Trust = \frac{R \times C \times I}{SO}$$

In this equation, R stands for **reliability,** C for **credibility,** I for **intimacy,** and SO for **self-orientation.** The first three elements correlate directly to trust, and have a multiplier effect. Conversely, however, self-orientation—which manifests itself as selfishness and narcissism—*undermines* trust.

Through such a framework, one can assess the development of trust in Code Halo initiatives.

- **Reliability:** Is your Code Halo reliable—and not just in a technical sense, but across your full business model? Are you consistently fulfilling expectations set for your customers?
- **Credibility:** Do your customers trust the information they find in your Code Halo—both direct information (such as pricing) and information derived through algorithm-based recommendations?
- **Intimacy:** Have you truly connected with your customer in your Code Halo at an individual level by providing customized, curated experiences? Or does your platform feel like an online "Dear Occupant" letter?
- **Self-Orientation:** There's little that's more alienating than working with a company and thinking, "Is this in *their* best interest, or mine?" Just as in personal relationships, any overt selfishness erodes trust. So, does your Code Halo focus primarily on its key constituents, or does your company keep forcing itself into each interaction?

The above equation is a useful construct for turning a concept as nebulous and unassailable as "trust" into something more quantifiable and actionable.

Perspective #4: The Law Will Never Catch Up

No discussion of the ethics of Code Halos could be complete without considering the legal implications and regulatory frameworks that currently or will exist. There is a huge body of literature that examines current Internet-related legislation and contains plenty of speculation about potentially forthcoming laws. We have no intention of rehashing or summarizing that material—partly because it would be impossible in this space, but mostly because it's unnecessary. It's highly unlikely that the practice of law will ever be able to operate at the warp speed of technology development. Laws and regulations will always lag current practice and will never fully anticipate future developments. None of the internationally regarded legal academics and experts to whom we put this proposition disagreed.

What does this mean for Code Halos? There is no material legislation that we know of—at least in the Western business world— that exists or is under development that would inhibit advancement of the scenarios we describe in this book. Certain countries and regions do have laws that will slow their development. German data privacy laws, for example, are among the most stringent in the world, so we would not advise you to start digging for Code Halo gold there. Then again, things change. Between 2000 and 2007, we heard objections to cloud computing and software as a service (SaaS) from many in Germany. But that resistance has waned and now some of the largest SaaS customers in the world are German companies.

In some other countries, particularly those suffering under repressive leadership, Code Halos are also unlikely to spark. Indeed, sharing the wrong personal information could be a life-threatening activity in certain places.

Legislation will be implemented, especially in developed countries, and this will be a positive development because new laws will help address some of the negative aspects of Code Halos. We are also likely to see best practices and industry norms emerging from trade bodies, industry groups, and analyst firms, all of which will provide useful frameworks for various aspects of ethics and privacy. In the absence of actual legislation, these voluntary codes of conduct will be adhered to by those seeking the high ground and ignored by everybody else. Ultimately, customer actions and economics will determine what weight these codes will carry.

The real question is: How can you, as a creator of Code Halo solutions, accentuate the positive and eliminate the negative?

Section II: Taking Action to Avoid Evil

We don't pretend to have all the answers to the ongoing security, privacy, and ethics issues that will emerge in the coming years—nor are we even able to articulate all the possible questions. But we can give you some straightforward steps to take in your organization to help ensure your operating practices stay on the side of what is commercially and ethically sound.

Below are a handful of tactical actions—illustrated with some scenario case examples to show how to act on these recommendations— that will help your organization embrace Code Halo thinking, while avoiding evil.

Action #1: Give Your Code Halo a Delete Button

Imagine that you work in a bank that has created a Code Halo solution for your wealth management customers. Your clients are receiving investment guidance through iPads with a proprietary— bio-encoded and secure—wealth management configuration, and your bank is enjoying accolades for maintaining personal-banker-centric service while allowing clients to customize their own experiences. You've used Code Halo thinking to change the wealth management game. You are learning more than ever about your customers, and they love the new service.

Except for Alice.

Alice is—or was—your perfect customer. She's interested in active wealth management, and happy to share her ideas, successes, failures, and questions with your bank's community. She's open to input, but also makes up her own mind, and she likes the fact that your bank is learning who she is, what her goals are, and how she likes to interact. She's mid-career, a member of a prosperous income bracket, and could be a terrific customer for decades to come. Then, one day, she sends a note to her virtual banker saying, "I'm changing jobs and banks. Please bundle my information, send it all to me, and then remove all of my information in your systems."

Alice's code—her history, what she liked, what she didn't like, her questions, her comments, for example—is of real value to you. You've learned how to grow your business with people like her, and this is a source of potential advantage. But setting aside the problem of retaining her as a customer, you now have to decide what to do with Alice's information. You technically own the data, but she's asked you to send her a copy and then delete it.

If you want to treat trust as your most important commercial asset in a Code Halo world—and you should—the answer is clear. But it has three parts.

1. **Retain what you must to comply with banking rules.** Banks, and many other industries, are subject to regulatory reporting requirements—many of which are always changing, complex, and expensive to follow. That's not going away, and nothing in Alice's request should have any impact on your normal adherence to these requirements. The only thing you should do differently based on her request is to **tell her what information you are going to retain.** And since you already know this, you won't have additional work or annoyance.

2. **Send her Code Halo back.** You have a solid business analytics engine running to collect, manage, and store the data associated with Alice and all your other customers. You have records of her messages, questions, answers, trades, likes, personal history, etc. So copy the files and send them back to her. You must be completely transparent with the data you have that originated with or relates to her.

3. **Hit the delete button.** Ask her to confirm her request. If Alice still wants to delete the files, you are ethically obligated to do so. You made money from Alice while she was a client, but she's

ending her commercial agreement with you, so you don't get to keep and use her data for future use. There may be metadata that is no longer possible to separate as "hers," but you should delete everything else as requested.

At this point you may be thinking a few things: "This sounds expensive." "It's impossible." "Nobody else is doing this." But these assumptions are wrong. Code Halo leaders are already operating on these principles.

Source: © Google

It probably won't come as a surprise that Google is leading the way in line with this specific recommendation. If you are a Google account holder, you can use its Takeout service to download a copy of your data right now. The solution is not perfect, nor does it work with all Google products, but it does embody the right ethical perspective in being transparent about data and creating a mechanism so account holders can get their data "back."[8]

Amazon also provides a convenient button to delete your browsing history. It is trying to act ethically by giving us—the people sharing our code with them—the red button to opt out.

Allow a Complete "Opt Out" to Maintain Trust

You may not work at a bank, but you will have a customer like Alice. To succeed in the world of Code Halos, you must allow your customers to leave. You are obligated to give back what you've been given, and be ready for people and organizations to "check out" when they want.

The counterclaim is that this competitive information was collected during the course of normal business. It costs the organization money to collect, analyze, and store that data. It's a legal competitive asset as much as a factory, barrel of oil, or retail store. This is correct, but the conclusion that you get to keep and use this data in perpetuity is not. Why? First, you didn't pay Alice for it. In fact, she probably wasn't even aware, initially at least, that you were collecting it. If you find a barrel of oil you want to use, but the owner steps up and says, "Hey, that's mine," and then produces a bill of sale, you give it back—all of it. You don't get to keep a few gallons because you want to. The same principles of this physical world reality hold true in the digital world. You are obligated to hit the delete button.

This means that you should keep in mind an exit plan that includes giving back a copy of someone's Code Halo—and then expunging this customer's records when requested. You may not want to, and it will sting a bit, but it's the only reasonable path to nurture trust—which is already becoming a key source of differentiation.

Action #2: Show Me You Know Me

Now imagine that you manage a big retail store chain. You've built a terrific omni-channel solution that allows customers to get in-store deals, link their online shopping experience with in-store visits, and even connect their credit card loyalty program with your brand. Your store—both physical and digital versions—is becoming a center for retail experience, rather than a big box with a parking lot. Steadily rising revenue per visit is one upshot.

Customers enjoy sharing their information with you because now you can instantly recognize them on arrival. Sales personnel can provide a more personalized shopping experience based on customers'

Code Halos. You're even starting to see evidence that this more intimate, service-oriented experience is helping to combat "show-rooming." As time passes, your data scientists are starting to draw insightful conclusions based on shopping patterns, and your team of behavioral scientists continues to find ways to refine your business analytics results.

The immense power of correlation is allowing different types of organizations to draw conclusions that seem like feats of magic.

Things were going great—that is, until Miranda came back into your central London store one day.

Miranda has been your customer for several years. She finished university a few years ago, and her online and in-store spend has increased roughly in line with her career growth. On the day in question, Miranda strode up to the customer service deck waving her personalized coupon for baby products. Angrily, she asked the assistant, "How did you know I'm pregnant?" and "What else do you know about me?" and then, "I want to speak to the manager."

Your Code Halo solution was working exactly as planned, but with a negative, unintended consequence. How should you respond to Miranda?

Retail has been in the business of aligning with customers since its inception. Learning about customers and selling to their wants and needs is Retail 101. What is new is the richness of insight—fueled by business analytics and meaning-making prowess—that Code Halos now makes possible. The immense power of correlation is allowing different types of organizations to draw conclusions that seem like feats of magic.

But if an organization now has the power to draw these conclusions, does it also have a new ethical obligation to *act* on these insights? Because every case is different, we break our answer into two parts.

The Responsibility to Be Proactive: What Do We Do If We Know?

If you are an insurance company, do you use your vehicle telematics device to turn off a car if the person shows signs of impaired driving? And what about medical professionals dealing with geriatric patients? In the UK and other places, they have a responsibility to advise on potential impairment—but it is the driver who initially has responsibility for acting on this information.[9]

In these cases, the driver is still personally responsible—not the car manufacturer, road builder, fuel company, media channel, etc.—until decisional authority is rescinded. In many U.S. states, if a person thinks a driver is no longer capable of making these decisions, there is a process for reporting potential issues to the Department of Motor Vehicles that can lead to a license being revoked.[10]

Of course, most organizations should not be policing or surveilling their customers; but our driving example emphasizes the importance of defining a path for what you'll do with new information and conclusions. In our impaired driver case, there's a fairly well-formed path for managing this process based on new data and insight such as, "Sorry, but now your vision is too poor for you to drive."

This matters for managers because there is one straightforward lesson from this to apply in your own context. For every major data investigation, have your data scientists answer the question: *"What will we do with our conclusions?"*

If you are a retail pharmacy with the ability to discern who has a debilitating condition or even a lethal illness, should you advertise specific health products? Medical management support? Family counseling? Estate planning? Funeral services? Some of these might be okay, while others are ghoulish and would rightfully damage your brand.

Code Halos make it necessary for organizations to wrestle with a fundamental question—*"What are we responsible for if we know?"*—before they start running analyses and looking for conclusions. Many are getting into hot water, facing criticisms around ethics and privacy, by failing to proactively address and answer this question.

In reality, the vast majority of these cases will be simple: If we see someone showing signs of seasonal allergies, we'll try to sell her over-the-counter medication. But the key here is to ask the question as a part of your business analytics processes.

The Burden of Response: What Do We Share?

Let's get back to Miranda. She specifically asked for information on how you are drawing conclusions about her. You need to do two things as a matter of ethical practice.

1. **Share your view of your contributors' Code Halos.** Similarly to what Google and Amazon are starting to do, you should be willing to share the data you collect about Code Halo participants. Organizations have a responsibility to reveal the data they have on customers, employees, partners, etc. when asked. Without this internal covenant in place, they move from being in the business of delivering valuable goods and services to the business of surveillance. This sets the wrong tone and direction for an organization not chartered to do so. And while this might not be characterized as *evil,* many customers *will* regard it as creepy.

2. **Share your meaning-making processes.** Business analytics is always in flux. People test things in different ways, draw new conclusions, have unplanned flashes of insight, etc. In the case of Miranda, the retailer probably didn't really comprehend *what* it knew about her—that is, how the insight it had generated from her purchases was taken as a devastating breach of privacy. However, *you* know how *you* are using data to make meaning and draw conclusions. This is why you should be ready to share the basics of this process. You don't necessarily have to share the details of a proprietary algorithm, or the aggregated results and conclusions that are helping your organization. But if someone sharing their Code Halo with you asks, "How did you know this?" you should be ready to give them a sense of how your meaning-making process works.

Action #3: Shine a Light on Your "Give-to-Get" Equation

Virtually every commercial transaction requires one party to give something—often money—to get something of value in return. This same principle applies to Code Halos, but what's being exchanged is often data—code—between partners. A customer, employee, or company will share information in return for value. A positive Give-to-Get ratio is one where the value of the code you provide about yourself (or that your system, process, or product provides about itself) is exceeded by the value of what you receive. Managing this trade-off transparently is essential to avoiding evil.

As an example, let's look at a life sciences scenario. Imagine you are a leader of an internal team at a pharmaceutical firm that has created a Code Halo solution that enables medical management for the millions of people with a potentially fatal peanut allergy (about 1.3% of the general population).[11] Your solution includes a mobile application interface for patients as well as medical care providers. Refill notifications are sent regularly, and data is flowing in from a growing community of patients and medical professionals, as well as research institutes and governing bodies like the U.S. Food and Drug Administration and the U.K. Food Standards Agency. The system is turning into a living, dynamic laboratory, with new research trends emerging based on shared experiences. You've just released a microsensor that integrates with a mobile device to test a food for hidden peanut toxins and are delivering this as a revenue-generating service but at a reduced price for program participants.

You know all about the Health Insurance Portability and Accountability Act (or HIPAA) and other regulations, and people have opted in to your program by signing up to share their data with you and others in return for information, community, remote monitoring, updates, etc. Now your customer José wants to leave the program, but only partially. He likes the updates and the lower monitoring costs, but he doesn't want to contribute his information anymore—and he's incensed and surprised when he's told that it's an all-in-or-all-out program.

So what went wrong? The obvious disconnect happened because of a lack of clarity—or understanding—of the Give-to-Get agreement.

To ensure this clarity exists and that trust remains, we recommend you implement four tactics covering the data participants are sharing with you and what they are getting in return.

1. **Tell me what you want; tell me what I'll get.** Be sure to tell people what they are getting into when they enter into the agreement. Guide them on the Code Halo data you will collect and use, and be clear and transparent on the benefits participants will enjoy. Our example provides a clear, comprehensive list of "gets." Also, note that this is not something you'll do only once. The data you want, and the value you deliver, will change over time. That's fine, just don't be coy about it. You'll still need legal-approved terms of service, and privacy policies, for instance. This is different. Be clear and open in a way *you yourself* would appreciate.

2. **Don't assume I read it.** Most of us are not lawyers, and all of us are inundated with legalese, policies, ads, surveys, spam, and more ads that all becomes electronic noise over time. That doesn't mean you should communicate more; it means communicate with the **greatest possible clarity and simplicity.** You're inviting others to participate in an exchange of data and value, so treat that interaction with some care. Communication is a two-way street, so merely stating your policy and then hiding behind your lawyer will not—and should not—create the level of trust you need.

3. **Make the relationship truly elective.** As we've discussed, the same consumer who freely elects to share his or her location on Foursquare may also feel enormously violated by unannounced surveillance from license plate scanning. Code Halo participants need to be able to elect in or out, *and at any time during the process*—not just the beginning. There should be no attempt to "game" this dynamic or make this election process more complicated than it need be. A failure to be open at this moment will likely backfire on you in a world of instantaneous social media sharing.

4. **Give me options for the terms of our endearment.** There are
   two main types of relationships you should plan on. The first
   is a transactional relationship where people have a commercial
   interaction, but they don't opt in to the enriched Code Halo
   solution. This should be fine with you. Perhaps, like some of us,
   you don't want an enriched personal interaction when you pick
   up a rental car; you just want the car, thanks. For other interactions, you may want a more intimate relationship, with deeper
   understanding and resulting higher value. The choice should be
   up to the participant, and it's your responsibility to be clear about
   the trade-offs. If someone opts for the pure transaction
   relationship, the person should know that she can't later come
   asking for the Code Halo treatment—at least, until she opts in.

Create an Opt-In Mentality

The Code Halo world will continue to grow, not only because people
are willing to accept the inherent risks, but because they will be
afforded more and better methods to control them. Integral to this
will be that Code Halo organizations should not use code without
explicit permission—that is, without a clear "opt-in" from the user.
They should also make it completely transparent just *what* it is the
user is "opting-in" *to*. In a world full of deliberately obscure and boring
legalese, users often click the *I Accept* button because life is too short.

---

*The Code Halo world will continue to grow, not
only because people are willing to accept the
inherent risks, but because they will be afforded
more and better methods to control them.*

Organizations should not bury key limitations, intentions, liabilities,
or caveats in the small print. It is safe to assume that consumers will
increasingly differentiate between providers' Code Halos based on the
nature and communication of opt-in policies. Organizations should
take this issue seriously, not blow it off as a boring eleventh-hour

contractual obligation, and realize that making this as readable and user-friendly as possible will be an important element of their overall value propositions.

Opting in and out will be the foundational principle of the Code Halo world; embrace and act on this zeitgeist.

Share the Code of Your Gives and Gets

The most important step is the most basic: Make your Give-to-Get ratio so rewarding that, in the same way that the cost and convenience of Internet era 1.0 triumphed over its doubters, the new Internet era of Code Halos will similarly see its detractors' voices diminish—and perhaps, someday, even disappear.

If people decide the value they're getting from the code collision is genuinely cool, fun, useful, meaningful—in sum, worth it—they will be prepared to opt in and live with the gives, and the potential downsides. If I can rebook my flight and hotel reservation in 30 seconds with a few clicks through Orbitz, I will accept the possibility my credit card details could get stolen. I'd rather live with that faint possibility than have to spend 10 minutes getting the numbers for Delta and Starwood, phoning a call center, entering booking numbers, holding for a few minutes, then explaining (probably more than once) what I need to do. That may be the safer way to do it, but it's a much more painful approach. And anyway, I'm giving my credit card to a total stranger on the phone in the longer-winded method too.

When there are manageable "gives" and positive "gets," opting in to a Code Halo connection is a no-brainer, and even the smartest—or most paranoid—brains will make that trade-off. Very simply, there are many cases where a person or organization is happy to relinquish some element of privacy and information to get something valuable in return. However, if it is imposed upon them—particularly surreptitiously—trust can be instantly and badly damaged; so clear, open communication about the trade-offs is the foundation for making this work.

Action #4: Calibrate Your Approach for a Global Stage

The good news is that the Internet allows your business to span the globe. The bad news is that your business can now span the globe.

Imagine, for example, that you have applied Code Halo thinking to a global campaign to reduce unplanned pregnancy, which has created a community of young people sharing personal information about their love lives. In some parts of the world, this is seen as normal and healthy; in others, you may be encouraging illegal acts. What do you say to a government authority enforcing laws you find objectionable that asks for the personally identifying information of your community? What if you are selling medical marijuana (legal in some places, not others)? What if you are running clinical drug trials that follow the legal conventions in one part of the world but not another? What if young students are using your platform—but their government wishes to seize such data and use it in ways you find objectionable?

Perhaps you hand over the data. Perhaps you do not. Unfortunately, there's no book, lawyer, consultant, regulator, or cleric that can answer all these questions for you. What you must do, however, is to have a plan for **who gets what information** if they come asking. It's essential to decide in advance what information you'll share, and under what circumstances.

Even though there is no single rule, we *do* have a starting point. We suggest that you design a few simple decision trees for requests that could come in from four different categories:

1. **Legal authorities and regulators:** If a civil or criminal entity with legitimate legal oversight of your organization requests information, and they follow their own appropriate processes—show up with a search warrant, subpoena, or other formal request for information—then you clearly have no choice but to hand it over. This includes auditors, police, inspectors general, regulating agencies, etc. You should not, however, help these agencies avoid or circumvent any processes or practices designed to govern the process. If they have a legitimate request, you should ensure that everyone follows the rules in place to manage that request.

2. **Code Halo ecosystem partners:** Code Halos frequently reveal insights that are of commercial interest to ecosystem partners. Because these friends of the firm will ask for such information, you need a planned response. Our recommendation is that you "show what you know" within the terms you should have already defined when you built your solution. That's a start; but new correlations will emerge over time that you'll need to manage on a case-by-case basis. Bear in mind that these requests are likely the foundation for an expanded commercial relationship. Jointly review the potential impact of sharing critical data, and assess whether there are new opportunities for value or whether this might damage trust with *your* customers. You should not just hand over information without going through this step.

3. **Internal associates:** Other internal teams or departments not directly involved in your Code Halo solution, but seeking to use data from it, should be treated as external partners. Although this can be a difficult situation to navigate and police, you only have to look at problems in other industries— banking, consulting, for example—to see what will likely happen without building some protective internal barriers. After all, your colleagues in these teams have not discussed or agreed to any of the things we've discussed here. By handing over information without working through a predefined process, you are breaking the agreements you've worked hard to set up with consumers, employees, partners, and customers.

4. **Entities with questionable or contested authority:** This is the category with the most drama—"Hey guys, a certain country called asking for personal data we think could be misused to identify potential political dissidents"—but it's the simplest process, since the answer is always "No." However, things get murky when you get a request that might be contested based on ethics from an entity with some authority. You are now in Edward Snowden and NSA territory. Facebook and others have been addressing this head-on, and so need to have their own teams interpreting what are reasonable requests.

Based on Facebook's own interpretations of federal
privacy laws, a warrant is only necessary to compel
disclosure of inbox and outbox messages less than
181 days old. Everything else can be obtained with
subpoenas that do not even require reasonable
suspicion. Accordingly, over the past six years,
government agents have worked the beat by mining the
treasure trove of personal and confidential information
on Facebook.[12]

This is, of course, getting Facebook in hot water with its users—
even though the NSA has over 40,000 "likes." You will not "solve"
this issue, and you'll ultimately have to manage these requests on an
individual basis. However, you should have a basic process in place
for what you do if your Code Halo information attracts this kind of
attention.

Action #5: Hard-Code Self-Control

Self-regulation by organizations will be a critical element of success in
a world of Code Halos. Groups from all sectors can learn here from
the medical profession's Hippocratic Oath, designed to help ensure
medical practitioners would "treat the sick to the best of one's ability,
preserve patient privacy, teach the secrets of medicine to the next generation, and so on."[13] Just as the Hippocratic Oath emerged millennia
before there was any such thing as the American or British Medical
Association, people and organizations of good faith will have to step
forward to do the right thing *because it is the right thing*—not just
because a politician or a lawyer or a journalist is watching.

Self-regulation will spring from the social mores that the new
digital native generation develop—mores of openness and accountability,
as well as control and disapprobation. Yes, we have seen the limitations
of self-regulation in many industries. It will be flawed and imperfect for
the foreseeable future, and bad things will occasionally happen.
Governments, regulators, and industry groups will move sluggishly to

address them. Debates will swirl endlessly. We will hear aggrieved cries of "Something must be done!" which will be answered by the question, "And what might that be?" Those with vested interests will agitate and organize.

Self-regulation by organizations will be a critical element of success in a world of Code Halos.

But through it all, people will continue to vote with their fingers and their wallets. As we perceive value and benefit, and as positive Give-to-Get ratios continuously reinforce Code Halo principles, we will jump forward, making things up as we go along.

Organizations using Code Halo approaches must ensure that, above all, they "do no harm"—and make their give much greater than their get in the absence of anyone telling them to do so. Here's how you can start the process.

Plan for Your First Internal Meeting

As you develop a Code Halo solution it will become apparent that when everything works as planned, you'll have a treasure trove of meaningful information to help you with the future of your work. You'll also conclude or remember that this means you have to start thinking about all the privacy, security, and ethics implications of knowing more. This is when you'll need to pull the right people together to start to build the structure for avoiding evil. It will be a recurring theme for you, but you should start with the inputs, processes, and outputs of your first Code Halo-focused meeting.

- **Inputs:** You should have the rough design for the solution as you go into your session. This should include the kinds of information you'll be collecting, a rough sketch of the anatomy elements of your solution (as described in Chapter 4), and the kinds of conclusions you may be deriving. You should have one slide on your process for meaning-making (so others can see how you'll convert data into insight). You should also, based on a scan of the market, summarize the other Code Halo solutions in the market or under development. You want to frame the list of key industry-aligned questions you have now, which you know are going to change over time. Lastly, you need a summary of what you think the implications could be for your organization regarding security, privacy, and compliance. These should be along the lines of our recommended actions: How will we "Show Me You Know Me"? How will we decide who gets what information, and when? What external regulations are relevant? Where are the big holes? One major question should be posed: How will we ensure we avoid evil with this solution?

- **Process:** The session should not be a squeezed 30 minutes, but a more considered half-day. Attendees should know they are there to work and engage, not park for a bit before lunch. Your very first action will be to guide the discussion away from becoming the "Committee of No." You are reengineering and innovating, and that requires taking risk. This group's job is to understand and manage that risk. Keep an eye out for people who want to revert to old thinking, those who will come up only with reasons why something "can't ever" happen. The bulk of the session should be spent workshopping—and taking action on—the items in your question list. Some attendees will be specific to your organization, but you should definitely include whoever is on point for: legal, privacy, risk, compliance, logical security, applications, business analytics, and enterprise architecture. You'll want to include others—HR, sourcing, finance, shared services, external partners for design, services, consulting, etc.—as required. Your subsequent meetings will be smaller; but it's preferable for the first discussion to err on the side of too many people than to leave out a critical voice.

- **Outputs:** Your goal is to begin to hard-code self-control into your organization around a new Code Halo solution and to begin to put privacy and ethics as a top consideration for all involved. You're using a cool new idea as a catalyst for change.

You want answers to some tactical questions, but it's more important to concur on "how" you'll do this than determining the "what" for a specific solution. Your number one output is a roadmap to keep "Don't Be Evil 2.0" ideas embedded in your Code Halo strategy. Remember, institutionalizing self-control is not a "one-and-done" session. It's a change to the organization that must be made for the sake of all involved. A big enterprise might have a large team of people focused on these issues, while a small car dealership may have only two or three. Start early, follow the plan, and focus on one step at a time. If you let things sit, or think this is not essential, then trouble awaits.

Be Proactive Early to Avoid Being Evil—and Creepy

As Code Halos proliferate, as people understand them better, and as they see evidence of the value they create, an entirely new ecosystem of value-added management services will develop around Code Halo connections. Many of these solutions will focus on security, privacy, and compliance. Over time, we will have apps to manage our code, dashboards to monitor and analyze them, and tools to customize our information for different interactions and situations. We might tailor our Code Halo such that company X knows us in some ways but not in others; that friend or colleague Y has access to every bit of information related to some parts of our lives but not all; and that organization Z can connect only with a very stripped-down version of our Code Halo. We will be able to manage and track third-party use of our data sets.[14]

Not every aspect of our new environment will be positive. However, the inherent nature of the Code Halo world—and the commercial incentives that exist for good behavior within it—makes us confident that, in the end, societies, organizations, and individuals will be able to figure out how to navigate a new social contract for the social network, and continue to pursue happiness in a world where code meets code. We clearly and unequivocally see this story as a "song of hope."

Code Halos are innovations; therefore, they will be messy, emergent, and unpredictable. You might assume from reading this section that you need to build a huge framework of processes associated with management and distribution of data, metadata, correlations, and algorithms, but that's not what we're saying. You just need to consider, in advance, how you'll share and manage data to keep your organization's ethical compass true. You don't need to overengineer, hire a cadre of lawyers, or paralyze yourselves worrying about what a certain government might or might not do. You do need to think about who may want your Code Halo data someday and consider how to handle those requests.

Bad Code Halo behavior will be instantly and widely known, and could push the miscreants toward an Extinction Event. For individuals, it could lead to banishment.

Openness will ultimately ensure the value of Code Halos, because it will mandate good behavior and accountability. Just as lousy service at a restaurant or retail venue or other service provider—which might have gone unnoticed or unpunished in the days before social media—is now broadcast with sometimes devastating impact, anyone who misuses or exploits the information exchanged via Code Halos will be exposed. Organizations will know that people will know if they transgress—and that those individuals won't want to share their information and enable connections with them. Organizations who violate these recommendations could lose customers, partners, and the opportunity to gather data and insight. Bad Code Halo behavior will be instantly and widely known, and could push the miscreants toward an Extinction Event. For individuals, it could lead to banishment.

You may be forgiven for mistakes in a Code Halo world—but you will not be forgiven for dishonesty. The cover-up truly will be worse than the crime.

With these essential points of view in mind, in the next two chapters we'll continue our exploration of the four principles of success in the Code Halo economy by examining how to manage your career based on code and by looking at how the IT function should be transformed to build and manage these new solutions. New times call for new attitudes and approaches, and a willingness to reexamine—and then act on—new operating principles. Success in the emerging Code Halo economy will be determined by those able to seize the imperative for change.

CHAPTER TEN

Manage Your Career Based on Code: Winning in the Wirearchy

When we work, where we work, how we work, who we work with, and how we manage are undergoing breakneck transformation thanks to the emergence of the Code Halo economy. Some elements of the traditional management process will remain intact, but others will change dramatically. This chapter looks at how management and leadership are changing in this environment and provides a series of recommendations on how *you* personally can successfully navigate in these new waters.

At their core, management and leadership are simply exercises in knowledge and communication. The SMAC Stack is naturally suited for a rich exchange of information and ideas. Yet most managerial structures, methods, and cultures are trapped in centuries-old approaches that ignore the power of these innovations and new mindsets about work. Learning these "new rules of code" will help you survive and thrive in a Code Halo world.

The Changing Nature of Power: Hierarchy versus "Wirearchy"

Regardless of size, industry, or location, most organizations currently manage through a command-and-control hierarchy. Though this worked for hundreds—if not thousands—of years, it's not working anymore. Millennials prefer to work in **heterarchies**—dynamic networks of connected nodes free of predefined priorities or ranks, like that shown in Figure 10.1.

Organizations Blend Hierarchy and Wirearchy Structures

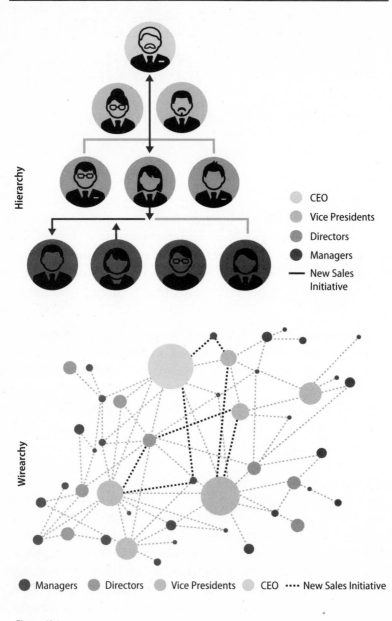

Figure 10.1

We can imagine this in the context of a digital organization as a "wirearchy." (The term "wirearchy" was coined and defined by the consultant and author, Jon Husband.[1])

Having grown up using social networks and collaborative platforms, Millennials recognize wirearchies instantly, choose to live in them, and can quickly locate the key players within them. Members of these networks earn status through knowledge and willingness to share. Unfortunately, many Millennials recognize that their organization operates completely out of sync with the way they want to work.

The org chart no longer represents power, the "go-to" people in an organization, or how employees conduct important work. The formal hierarchy is misaligned, and often conflicts with, the realities of the wirearchy. Making partner or becoming a vice president in a wirearchy are no longer final destinations or proof that you've "made it." This dissonance is highly destructive to the organization's morale and, eventually, performance. Highly qualified Millennials are starting to vote with their feet by opting to work at companies that truly and overtly value wirearchies. Organizations can no longer afford to ignore this trend. *You need to make sure you are an active part of the community in the wirearchy.* As Woody Allen said, "80% of success is showing up."[2]

Now, will hierarchies disappear? Of course not. The best model is a hybrid of the two, balancing formal org chart power with more informal wirearchy authority. In the coming decades, the most effective managers will be those who consciously live in both physical and virtual power structures.

The question then becomes "What belongs in the hierarchy, and what then moves to the wirearchy?" This chapter endeavors to answer that question in two sections. First, we'll outline some warning signals: "You know you're in trouble when…." These signals indicate when traditional approaches are no longer working. Then our second section provides six rules for success within the new organizational model:

1. **The Deming Rule:** Use data to end HIPPO management.
2. **The Rule of Virtual Work:** Out of sight, front of mind.
3. **The Tattoo Rule:** Manage your professional Code Halo.
4. **The Keyser Söze Rule:** Does your online reputation precede itself?
5. **The Node Rule:** It's not all about you.
6. **The Value-Add Rule:** Don't regurgitate. Create!

Section I: You Know You're in Trouble When ...

It's understandable that many will feel uncomfortable during this era of transition, and will no longer feel aligned with their organization's operating style. To that end, we've described below some signs of personal trouble in navigating the wirearchy—and recommendations on how to course-correct. If you aren't facing these challenges and are already doing many of these things, great. If you're not, it's time to start (and there is time to succeed). Whether you are 25 or 55, doing well in this new reality is not a function of age; it's about adopting the best practices and mindset for new ways of working.

You're Uncomfortable with "Scrambled-Egg" Life

Twenty years ago, most all of us lived a "fried-egg" life. Work was the egg's yolk, and your personal life was the white portion surrounding it. The two worlds sat in equilibrium, but they didn't really mix, and there was a distinct line between the two components. Work was work, and home was home.

More of us in today's organizations are living a "scrambled-egg" life: a mix of work and personal life where the lines between the two have become very blurred. At home, we're often returning emails from bed late into the evening, or engaged on a videoconference in the living room. Similarly, we may take a break to schedule a child's dentist appointment or do some online holiday shopping during the traditional "workday."

Those who master the scrambled-egg life become more effective and efficient workers and better family members as well. But this trend also comes with ongoing ambiguity. You may have a Saturday morning team video call, but you can also go for a run at 1 p.m. on Thursday.

For some, this is business as usual; for others, it's a difficult transition. It's time to embrace this new balance. In some ways, your job will never feel completely done, for you can't "leave work" as you could in the fried-egg world. Thus, instead of bemoaning the intrusions and downsides of scrambled-egg life, also remember—and actively manage—the efficiencies and work-balance flexibility it can provide. After all, you have no one to blame but yourself if you only accept its downside but don't protect and utilize its upside.

A Computer Can Tell You What to Do

The next time you drive through an E-ZPass toll sensor, remember a person used to be standing there. Think hard about whether you may one day be E-ZPassed on your current professional path. Very simply, if a computer can tell you what to do, you're in long-term career trouble. However, you're on a great path if you can tell a computer what to do. In other words: *Make sure you're writing the algorithm, rather than just responding to it.*

We're already seeing some hard realities of the Code Halo economy. Over the past generation, technology has had a painful, wrenching impact on blue-collar employment for many. We will see similar impacts on white-collar employment in the coming generation. A key line of demarcation—between those made redundant by technology, and those made more influential—comes in your ability to tell the computer what to do.

You Hate Social Media and Never Skype

Perhaps you think people posting on Facebook are just wasting time. You use your landline to catch up with your overseas friends rather than Skype them. You don't have a LinkedIn profile. You signed up for Twitter but don't use it, and have forgotten your password. If this sounds familiar, you're really going to hate the organization of 2020.

Remember the travel advisory: "If you don't like the food of a country, you probably won't enjoy visiting there." Whether you decide to vacation in Chile or China is elective. However, working in virtual networks is becoming core curriculum.

If all of this seems foreign, start learning—fast! Try "reverse mentoring." Enlist a tech-savvy (often younger) colleague, friend, or family member to teach you the language of their virtual world and show you how engaging using Instagram, Vine, or ooVoo can be. Once you've seen this world through their eyes, you can start exploring.

Golf Is Central to Your Sales Strategy

Relationship building is and will remain essential to connecting goods and services to customers. But if golfing, or Formula 1 seats, or an NFL skybox are the only arrows in your quiver, it's probably an indication that you aren't truly engaging with your customers.

You build and nurture deep, trust-based connections more effectively when you combine virtual connections with physical interactions.

Sharing information and connecting virtually will lead to more consistent engagement—the kind that takes you beyond prior years' more "episodic" interactions. Not to knock golf, but the sport is losing its relevance in business. Nowadays, it's where the older suits go to support their personal interests—rather than their employers'.

We have nothing against traditional relationship-building activities. We are all still people who thrive on personal connections. However, playing golf *in lieu* of virtual relationship management is now a losing game. You build and nurture deep, trust-based connections more effectively when you *combine* virtual connections with physical interactions. You can certainly still take clients to the golf course, but that should not be the foundation of your sales strategy; yours or your organization's.

Section II: Rules for Personal Success in the Wirearchy

In analyzing how work and career paths will change due to the rise of Code Halos, we've developed six rules that are crucial to successfully managing yourself at the Crossroads.

The Deming Rule: Use Data to End HIPPO Management

Gary Loveman, the former Harvard Business School professor who has revolutionized the gaming industry by bringing analytics to Caesar's Entertainment Corporation, is fond of saying, "[T]here are three ways to get fired from the hotel and casino company: theft, sexual harassment, and running an experiment without a control group."[3]

We know by now that Caesar's is by no means unique. It's now imperative to hold yourself and your team accountable to a data-driven method of management by leveraging the massive amount of data swarming around you and your business processes. Managers have traditionally had to manage in the absence of good data—or any data at all. Because of this, management has been—by necessity—typically an act of opinion: "It is my belief that we should do x." And in a standoff between opinions, the more senior employee usually carries the day. The **H**ighest **P**aid **P**erson's **O**pinion has traditionally been the one that mattered.

But management by HIPPO is under attack in a Code Halo world. HIPPOs will soon be on the endangered list. Code Halo type organizations—like Google, whose analytics guru Avinash Kaushik coined the very term—are leading the hunt for HIPPOs.[4]

You should trust the data and the algorithm as Google did, and see that it becomes unacceptable in your organization for decisions to be made on gut instinct, a sense—opinion—alone. Implement the following ideas to lead with data:

- **Create a heuristic for generating data.** Develop repeatable rules and patterns for your people to build and source data. Tell your team precisely what data they should capture, where they will find it, and how they should go about collecting it. Show that you value this approach by promoting the people who become consistent data "hounds."

- **Democratize your key data.** You have data; share it! DJ Patil—VP of products at RelateIQ and formerly Chief Scientist at LinkedIn—recommends making your sales metrics, delivery metrics, production metrics, and financials available to everyone in your organization. Even if it's uncomfortable. By making it *available*—even in a small way—you are helping to emphasize the point that information matters more than an unfounded opinion in your organization.
- **Focus on the code of your Code Halo solution.** You should make decisions related to Code Halo solutions *based on data*. As soon as your new solution is operational, you must become obsessive about collecting and analyzing any data that it starts to generate. Clearly indicate the importance of this data to your teams by making developmental decisions based on it.

Hold both yourself and your team to the discipline of being data-driven in decision-making.

The key is working with your team to determine your own data management supply chain; what data is important to you, how is it captured, what lenses (e.g., analytics and reports) do you utilize to "manufacture" it, and is it utilized—and even enforced—in key portions of your management process. Hold both yourself and your team to the discipline of being data-driven in decision-making.

The Rule of Virtual Work: Out of Sight, Front of Mind

Building long-term, trust-based relationships by virtual means sounds like an oxymoron—but it's not. However, you want to adhere to a few key elements to make sure things go well:

- **Be available—and make sure people know it.** Initially, working virtually may feel more interruption-driven than in-office work. Your videoconference machine will pop on, and a face from 1,000 miles away will be staring at you. Three instant messages will come in during a conference call. At times, it will feel a bit chaotic. However, being available—whether by videoconference, email, phone, chat, or texting—is essential to leading virtually. Some managers initially push back on the idea of a scrambled-egg life becoming reality. Remind yourself not only of the efficiencies gained—flights, meetings, and long email debates avoided—but more important, the value of a management process that can be greatly accelerated.

- **Manage and collaborate by beaming around.** Commit to going *virtual* first—in other words, defaulting to the videoconference as the platform for meeting. It means looking for the right person for the job, regardless of physical location when you launch a new project. So which technologies are key? First, using a videoconferencing service is a must—whether on a sophisticated company network, or by leveraging inexpensive third-party platforms such as Skype, ooVoo, iChat, or others. Managers who adopt videoconferencing often refer to it as a "killer app." When William Hewlett and David Packard were running HP, they popularized the concept of "Management by Walking Around." Senior leaders were able to meet with the majority of their divisions and managers simply by physically visiting their offices or the cafeteria in Silicon Valley. Today, this approach is giving way to the concept of "Management by Beaming Around." This is the only way (so far) to visit teams, clients, and candidates in Mumbai, Paris, London, Toronto, and New York … all by noon.

- **Hold off-site and mandatory in-office days.** You cannot fight human nature; people need to *get together* to build deep relationships. Following the rhythm of quarterly off-site meetings—with both work and social time—will facilitate these virtual connections. Also, mandate certain in-office days—but ensure true interaction occurs during those days with meetings, workshops, and customer sessions.

The Tattoo Rule: Manage Your Professional Code Halo

In the physical world, most of us give great care to how we appear to others. It's why we get certain haircuts, groom ourselves, buy nice clothing, work out, pay attention to our manners, and act ethically. But are you paying similar attention to your virtual appearance and reputation?

Spend the first day of the month looking into your virtual mirror to see yourself as others see you.

How do you go about managing your own Code Halo? The first and most obvious step is another variation of the previously discussed Hippocratic Oath: "do no harm." That is, no posting of embarrassing party photos, no political or societal rants. It's never a good idea to drink and type. Before you put more ink onto your virtual tattoo[5]—which, like real tattoos, often don't age well—ask yourself, "How would I feel if this were put on the front page of *The New York Times*? Or Buzzfeed?" If the answer isn't a quick "I'd have no problem with that," then it's best to stop typing.

You also obviously need to build the positive qualities of your Code Halo. Spend the first day of the month looking into your virtual mirror to see yourself as others see you. Google, Bing, LinkedIn, Facebook, and Twitter yourself, and spend a few minutes reviewing what people have posted. After all, this is what your colleagues, customers, business partners, and next prospective employers—internally or externally—are doing. What did your search uncover? Do you see your half-marathon times, political contributions, and an unfortunate photo from your high school reunion? Or do you see the arc of your career, a mosaic of your unique capabilities, others lauding your talents and accomplishments? If you see the former, you have work to do. Clean up what you can control: update your LinkedIn and Twitter profiles—in particular, with a network effect of third-party testimonials.

Take the time to actively manage your virtual professional self.

Remember the two currencies of virtual communities: **trust** and **content.** Both are rich words. Where trust is concerned, ask yourself: are you punctual, fair-minded, transparent, collaborative, open, honest, and focused on delivering quality work with consistency? And in terms of content—do you have recognized subject-matter expertise in whatever is your field of choice? Whether right or wrong, fair or unfair, those who exhibit trust and provide high-value content in virtual networks are quickly rewarded. In a flywheel effect, a reputation on these two elements can build upon itself quickly in virtual networks—both positively and negatively. Take the time to actively manage your virtual professional self.

The Keyser Söze Rule: Does Your Reputation Truly Precede Itself?

Once you've managed your personal Code Halo, you can then take it to the next level. We call this the Keyser Söze rule, after the legendary underworld boss from the film *The Usual Suspects* who cultivated a reputation that enabled him to alter events and persuade those who had never even laid eyes on him. Similarly, do your reputation and influence extend far beyond your physical reach? If you're managing effectively in a wirearchy, they should. Admittedly, it may be a bit extreme to compare yourself to an archcriminal like Söze, but it highlights an important point: in wired organizations and markets, your reputation greatly precedes your presence.

As we mentioned in Chapter 9, Warren Buffett famously said, "It takes 20 years to build a reputation and five minutes to ruin it. If you think about that, you'll do things differently." This has been true forever; our reputations have preceded us for thousands of years. What's new with technology is that we share information—facts, myths, rumors—faster and more broadly than ever before. Good behavior—honesty, trust, great delivery, generous acts of mentorship—and bad behavior—arrogance, blowing people off, poor delivery—don't just travel by word of mouth. They are all shared and written in digital "stone." Ensure your network knows who you are, what you expect of its members, and how to best engage with you.

The Node Rule: It's Not All About You

Because a hierarchy prioritizes the top of the pyramid, it ultimately celebrates the *individual*. A wirearchy is a network, so it instead prioritizes the *node*. As such, it celebrates the networker who sits at an important hub, that generous spirit who gives more than he or she receives, who focuses on others' success.

There are several simple tests you can use to judge your effectiveness as an important node in the network. The best test is to ask yourself: Do you have too much email, seemingly being included on everything, or is your inbox easy to manage? If it's the former, that's a good sign. If it's the latter, that's bad, for wirearchies are often like pickup basketball games: similar to that lineup of potential players on the fence next to the basketball court. If you're not being picked for a team, it's because others simply don't want you on their team. Instead of seeing how high you've climbed up the corporate ladder, it's better to check how quickly your inbox fills up.

Today's leading MBA programs prioritize collaboration as a key factor of future managerial success. This bodes well for future organization leaders, but for those of today, a daily reminder of "team first" over "me first" will serve one well.

The Value-Add Rule: Don't Regurgitate; Create!

The Node Rule doesn't simply mean you should be passing information from point A to point B, pushing virtual paper. Instead, it means you should be providing value, creating meaning, at each opportunity. Do this in each interaction, and you'll never be replaced with technology.

Consider high school as a corollary: if you regurgitated information in a perfect manner, you'd get a good grade. At a prestigious college however, simply regurgitating information will get you no more than a "gentleman's C." Top grades are reserved for those who think, synthesize, and create. Similarly, you don't just forward that email when you're working in a virtual, networked organization. You need to synthesize it, provide insight, create—and add value.

Act Now to Thrive in the Organization of 2020

The rules for personal success in the wirearchy are different from the best practices of past decades. If you're acting on these six rules you're no doubt in great shape. You're probably already winning in the wirearchy. However, if you're still having fried eggs before you head out to the golf course it is imperative that you recalibrate aspects of your work life for the new world we're in and to avoid your own personal Extinction Event, which will not be pretty.

In the next chapter, we examine another aspect of the foundation of Code Halos, technology, and provide guidance on how enterprises should reconfigure IT to make it, once again, a competitive weapon.

CHAPTER ELEVEN

Make IT Your Halo Heroes: Transform Your Technology Organization

Most of us delight in our Sunday evening consumer technology experiences—video-chatting with friends, relaxing with Netflix, listening to music on Pandora. But when we arrive at work on Monday morning, we find our technology experience archaic, limiting—and even *lame*. As a result, many internal IT organizations are dealing with a credibility crisis that was not of their making. Over the past few years, while IT has been dutifully ensuring that the software and hardware was working effectively, efficiently, and securely, the consumer technology market caught fire. As a result, most organizations' information technology function is moving through its own version of the Crossroads Model. Many business leaders are wondering what they should expect from IT. Many, perhaps most, IT professionals are now also wondering what the future will hold.

There has been talk of "strategic computing" for years, but it's something many market observers thought of as self-congratulatory hyperbole. Business and technology writer Nicholas Carr famously stated "IT Doesn't Matter" in a 2003 edition of the *Harvard Business Review*.[1] When he wrote that, the notion may have been open for debate. Carr was right that some aspects of technology are simply cost centers or, at best, offer competitive parity. However, in the context of today—when SMAC technologies are directly infused into most every product and customer experience—the debate is firmly over. In the world of Code Halos, the business is now technology and technology is the business.

This shift presents a once-in-a-lifetime opportunity for "Halo Heroes" to step forward and lead their organizations to new levels of corporate performance. Rather than responding defensively ("Well, that all sounds great. We see the vision as well. But we don't have the skill sets to design and build consumer experiences.") some IT leaders are taking a different path by successfully leaning into their business and leading the charge to create a digital enterprise. They are reinventing their toolbox, upgrading their contribution, and not waiting for someone to tell them what to do. Many are taking the following three specific actions to make IT their "Halo Heroes"—and you can do the same:

1. **Structure IT for success.** Deploy the Three-Horizon Organizational Model—which we'll cover in detail later in the chapter—within IT.
2. **Find the budget.** Self-fund the transition.
3. **Fuse technology and business to win the New Code Rush.** Create a new model of interdependence between IT and the business.

This chapter outlines the steps required to transition IT—the discipline, the skill set, the business unit—from being a support function to a truly strategic weapon.

Action #1: Align IT Along Three Horizons

We have seen from our work with companies all over the world how many internal IT organizations recognize that they're currently on an unsustainable path—and now need to deliver against a "dual mandate."

1. Continue to execute on efficiency and scale with **existing systems.**
2. Drive business innovation through **newer technologies.**

IT is not blind to this challenge. In fact, many IT organizations would love to lead the charge on SMAC technologies in the workplace. But without the budget, time, and resources, leaders are forced to answer, "Sorry, we can't" more often than "Yes, we can." This generates friction—even conflict—with business leaders who need to innovate.

For example, we have seen IT teams from several leading car manufacturers in this bind. In each case, the business teams—from CXOs to product managers, engineers, and marketing—have seen the potential of SMAC technologies for cars and have informed IT: "Our cars need to become rolling computers. We need to connect onboard components to the Internet. We must enhance and personalize the driver and passenger experiences, with the dashboard becoming more like a tablet." In short, they want to build Code Halos around both the cars and their customers.

As much as IT may want to respond to this mandate, they are crushed by the daily demands of the current legacy environment. How do they manage not only the very different skill sets, but also differing cultural norms, under one roof? How do they get a team that is well steeped in operational efficiency, standardization, and serving existing business needs, which can also deliver on innovation related to new consumer needs?

Many IT organizations are paralyzed by the formidable challenge of executing against this dual mandate. So how can you break this organizational logjam?

One tactic is to employ the Three Horizons Model of portfolio management. Though increasingly well known in corporate strategy circles, this approach is just starting to find application in IT. Originally developed by consultants Mehrdad Baghai, Stephen Coley, and David White (and published in their 1999 book, *The Alchemy of Growth*), the model was an attempt to help organizations struggling to foster growth within their product and/or service portfolio.[2] At a business level, companies felt trapped in the "Innovator's Dilemma," unable to capture future innovations while still delivering on today's needs.[3] As shown in Figure 11.1, breaking work into three horizons has helped leaders segment how they create value:

- **Horizon One (H1)** represents parts of the organization focused on areas that once created competitive distinction, but are now competitive "table stakes." Such capabilities continue to be mission-critical—the firm could not survive without them—but they have reached a relative level of maturity and standardization.
- **Horizon Two (H2)** covers products or services that are established in the market but not yet at full maturity or commoditized. They comprise the bulk of revenues and continue—in many places—to provide competitive distinction.
- **Horizon Three (H3)** business offerings are the new, "next gen" offerings—those that show promise but are not yet proven and need time to take root. These are often "high beta" opportunities; that is, they have significant potential upside, but also relatively high chances of failure.

Three Business Horizons[4]

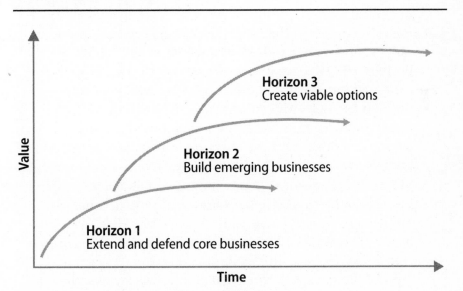

The original Three Horizons Model from *The Alchemy of Growth*, by Mehrdad Baghai, Stephen Coley, & David White, 1999, New York, Orion.

Source: McKinsey & Company

Figure 11.1

When applied to today's enterprise IT, the Three Horizons approach aligns technology teams to the distinct challenges, responsibilities, goals, and management styles required to succeed in a Code Halo world in the following ways:

- **H1 builds the foundation.** This includes the foundation of IT operations—corporate networks, email and messaging systems, and infrastructure. The company could have a "CNN moment" if these components go down. Yet as necessary as they are, these capabilities do not provide *competitive distinction*. The objective for H1 IT is to manage with a utility mindset: standardize, commoditize, build one-to-many systems, be efficient and always available, and strive for "good enough."

- **H2 builds the business.** This includes your "money maker" systems—often, standard enterprise applications such as the ERP backbone, front office CRM solutions, eCommerce platforms, and financial systems. Also included are industry-focused solutions, such as trading desks in investment banking, or clinical trials platforms in life sciences. These systems drive the vast majority of the company's current revenues. Some are unique, others are standard, all are critical. H2's focus is business effectiveness. Management faces the challenge of running these systems in tight alignment with your core business processes while preventing costs from inching up. These technologies can also contribute toward gaining competitive advantage, but gains are usually incremental (and often approach a point of diminishing returns).

- **H3 builds the future.** This is dominated nowadays by driving business and technical innovation with SMAC technologies. H3 teams conceive, build, and manage Code Halo solutions. Many H3 team members are—or should be—embedded within the business. This team should be your Code Halo "special forces"; small teams that you can deploy quickly who are looking for big results with limited resources. They should be experts on new technologies (the SMAC Stack) and deployment methodologies (Agile Development, Rapid

Prototyping, and Minimum Viable Products.[5]) These teams are your "eyes and ears"—constantly on the hunt for technical breakthroughs as well as innovative uses of technologies across your competitors and other industries.

Align the Charter and Goals for IT by Horizon

The Three Horizons Model allows organizations to clearly see which parts of IT are catalysts of the future and which are more focused on the here and now. Central IT—focused on H1 and H2—should become a smaller and smaller group over time. H1 roles should be primarily focused on sourcing and managing external services. H2 roles will include a broader mix of technical and sourcing skills; but here again the emphasis should be on leveraging external services where possible and only retaining in-house technical development skills for clearly differentiating custom systems. H3 team members should focus on SMAC Stack solutions and Code Halos.

Expectations, metrics, and management styles will be different for each horizon (see Figure 11.2).

Three Horizons of IT

Horizon Group	Containing	Charter	Metrics
One	Data centers, server management, network infrastructure, desktop management, bespoke legacy applications, printing, communications.	Cost center, cost reduction, competitive parity, efficiency, end of lifecycle management (e.g., of personnel, tech).	Service level agreement (SLA), uptime, availability, cost per transaction, CPU minute, budget reduction, FTE reduction.
Two	ERP applications, business COTS, technical COTS, competitively differentiating custom applications.	Support function, cost containment, competitive advantage, system effectiveness, upgrade cycle synchronization, personnel re-skilling, alignment with operational business units (e.g., finance, HR).	SLA, cost per transaction, service charge back, cost transfer, budget stabilization, return on investment.
Three	SMAC Stack technologies, design, IoT.	Strategic weapon, business value growth, competitive advantage, alignment with customer- and product-focused business units (e.g., design, engineering, marketing).	User adoption, new product introductions, number of favorable analyst/media mentions, revenue growth, data volume.

Figure 11.2

Sometimes this transition will require tough choices, particularly regarding IT department veterans whose careers have thrived by deploying and managing legacy systems. They may be emotionally tied to these tools and still think of them as distinctive. But you must escape this trap and remind these associates that, over time, these systems have standardized and commoditized. While they're still necessary, they no longer provide competitive advantage. Coke won't beat Pepsi because of its corporate network or HR systems. As such, these systems should be consolidated, standardized, rock-solid, and as cheap as possible.

Rebalance Your Leadership Focus to Match New Requirements

Making this shift successfully requires a rebalance of the leadership focus across different IT functions within each horizon. Application work remains relatively constant through this transition, but there is a dramatic difference between H1 and H3 activities. The user interface—in fact more accurately, the user "experience"—and the focus on data should greatly expand, while the focus on infrastructure should contract significantly, as shown in Figure 11.3.

Rebalancing Leadership Time in the Future IT Department

IT Element	Leadership Time and Focus	
	Legacy IT Department	**Code Halo IT Department**
User Interface	5%	30%
Application	30%	30%
Data	15%	30%
Infrastructure	40%	10%

Figure 11.3

Some people misperceive the Three Horizons Model as a celebration of H3 at the expense of the other two horizons, when nothing could be further from reality. Process orchestration, security, testing, master data management, application integration, enterprise architecture, compliance, service governance, product and services sourcing—and a long list of other roles and responsibilities—are essential for *any* business, Code Halo-focused or not, to do well. CMOs, design or engineering heads—even next-generation ones—have little interest, time, skills, or experience in managing core IT, and quite rightly so. They may be choosing the cloud-based customer experience solution and specifying the requirement, but they won't and *shouldn't* be concentrating on the things that only IT is genuinely qualified to manage.

Much of the work at the heart of Code Halos involves things that only "core IT" can do well.

The goal of this action is to put the right things in the right place to let the organization multitask effectively—essentially, to walk and chew gum at the same time. Importantly, central IT still remains foundational for all horizons of IT and for most Code Halo initiatives. Much of the work at the heart of Code Halos involves things that only "core IT" can do well. Enterprise IT must therefore rethink the organization to free up time and focus to drive innovation.

Action #2: Fund Your Own Transition

The natural question whenever a major IT change is proposed is, "Who pays for it?" As expected, a number of different answers circulate within most organizations. Some expect that the business will pay for all of it. After all, there have been several analyst reports predicting that the marketing budget for technology will exceed the IT budget in several industries in the coming years.[6] Others argue that the funding must come from IT itself. If the spend is not centralized, many worry that initiatives such as bring-your-own-device (BYOD) and cloud-based applications procured by business groups will soon spin wildly out of control. This could leave the organization with an unmanageable—and ultimately expensive and risky—hodgepodge of technology.

We believe that the middle road is the one to follow: for central IT and the business to work together to form a new model of collaboration, even one of interdependence, through which they jointly deliver the new initiatives and the new H3 organization. After all, the very nature of Code Halos means that they're embedded in the business. Yet at the same time, the technology requirements—in Big Data, integration with legacy systems, security, and systems management—require robust technology capabilities which only central IT can provide.

That leads us back to the budget. Many in the C-Suite still remember the "extortion schemes" of Y2K spending, Internet-bubble spending, and failed ERP backbone projects. Asking for significant additional IT funding for Code Halos—prior to proving their worth—is fraught with danger. While business units may come up with their own technology budgets, IT organizations need to find a way to bring cash to the table to—at least partially—"self-fund" the transition to a Three Horizons Model. Finding a way to free up investment will help IT keep control of its resources and destiny.

Attack the 80-20 Rule to Fund Innovation

Currently, most IT shops leave about 80% of their corporate IT budget and resources trapped, funding the installed base of systems and software, leaving only 20% for new technologies and initiatives. Too many IT organizations allocate an inordinate, and often growing, portion of their budgets to critical but nondifferentiating infrastructure and maintenance. Key to self-funding—and thus maintaining control—is to move to a budget profile in which infrastructure and maintenance savings then fund innovation. IT leaders who want to succeed need to rearrange the current 80-20 dynamic. The big question, of course, is "how?"

Drive Efficiencies in H1 and H2 IT

Driving the 80-20 equation to something more like 60-40 will double the budget for Code Halo initiatives. The first step is to create efficiencies in existing H1 and H2 IT resources and programs. There are many levers to pull.

- **Consolidate enterprise applications.** While the backbone of enterprise applications—ERP, CRM, HRM, and SCM systems—is essential to the company's daily operations, we rarely derive competitive advantage from it. Does your organization need multiple instances of several applications? No. We've seen radical simplification of the enterprise application backbone as key to driving efficiencies without sacrificing business effectiveness.

- **Move infrastructure to the cloud.** It's no longer acceptable to hide behind perceived security risks. In virtually every organization, some applications and core infrastructure can move to cloud partners who can manage assets better, faster, and cheaper. Such moves can also transition certain capital expenditures to operating expenditures, providing budget flexibility. Tactical systems such as expense management, HR, sales force automation (SFA), CRM, storage, and email are good candidates for many organizations.

- **Externalize services.** Leveraging the capabilities, scale, and global talent pools of external service providers is another tool for lowering the cost of your legacy environment. Why maintain legacy systems when service providers have deep experience and cost leverage that individual organizations cannot deliver? In many cases, hanging on to nondifferentiating capabilities is like carrying around a cost anchor you can't put down.

Many IT leaders will assert that they are already taking these steps. Most already have; but our market observations, supported by countless studies, suggest there are still huge opportunities for many firms to free up new IT budget quickly. In creating this budget headroom, IT organizations no longer need to look at SMAC-based requests with trepidation. They can begin to build the H3 competencies that they need—not merely to remain relevant, but to drive the entire organization forward.

Action #3: Tear Down the Wall Between IT and the Business

Organizations leading the Code Halo race have no barriers between IT and the business. They provide fantastically exciting roles and career paths for next-generation IT leaders. These individuals sit at the table along with product management, finance, engineering, and design specialists, and work with peers to develop frontline products and services.

However, most of these companies had a different starting point than the average organization, because they were *born digital*. For more established organizations aspiring to move in this direction, the Three Horizons Model is crucial to tearing down the wall that still exists between IT and the business.

Organizations leading the Code Halo race have no barriers between IT and the business.

Analysts and industry observers have for years recommended that IT become more closely aligned to the business. We're recommending that IT now actually becomes *part of the business*. This new model is aligned by horizon. H1 and H2 IT continue to be largely centralized functions, similar to what many organizations have today. However, as shown in Figure 11.4, the H3 component will look drastically different.

A New Federated Structure for IT (The Birthday Cake Model)

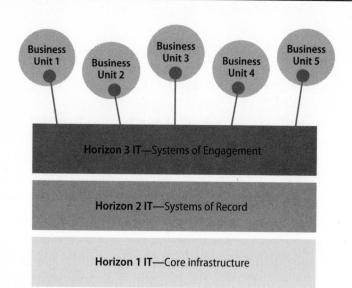

Figure 11.4

A portion of the H3 organization will remain centralized to manage the enterprise-wide issues associated with SMAC Stack technologies and Code Halo implementations. After all, the majority of Code Halo implementations will require integration between the old and the new; think of the auto insurance telematics device that needs to connect back to the customer's policy. This centralized H3 group focuses on issues such as: enterprise architecture, enterprise mobility, Big Data initiatives (which transcend the entire organization), security and— very importantly—integration of Code Halo systems of engagement, H2 corporate systems of record, and H1 core infrastructure.

This centralized H3 IT group will also house centers of excellence on H3 capabilities that currently do not exist within H1 and H2 IT. These functions are your in-house digitization organization, and include:

- **Design,** particularly focused on consumer IT interfaces for Code Halo amplifiers and interfaces.
- **Algorithm generation and management,** to centralize best practices on developing, updating, and managing your organization's algorithms.
- **SMAC center of excellence,** through which a core team would continually look at advancements in not only social, mobile, analytics, and cloud technologies, but also wearable computing, 3D manufacturing, and the Internet of Things. This group also sets corporate standards and policies for such technologies, builds new enterprise architecture models, and manages H3 provider relationships.

The Business-Embedded Portion of the New H3 IT Organization

The remainder of the H3 organization—which, over time, will be the majority of the group—will be colocated in the business units that drive particular Code Halo initiatives. These H3 staff members, represented in Figure 11.4 by the small circles within the business units, should sit close to the product managers who are upgrading existing products and services, as well as seeking new breakthrough thinking. For example, product managers at Nest would focus on specific Nest thermostats or smoke detectors. At Nike, it's people worrying about the Nike+ FuelBand. These hybrid IT/BU people should help product managers understand the possibilities of next-generation Code Halo-related technologies by working on aspects of the following:

- **Code Halo anatomy:** The joint team should focus on understanding the anatomy of the new Code Halo. They should define what the amplifier is—aka devices within the Internet of Things—and how it should function. They should plan the user interface aesthetic, define its usability, and orchestrate the end-to-end solution.
- **Code Halo data and analytics:** Driven by the H3 resource, the team should dig deep into what data can be created by use

of the device or service. They should be responsible for deriving maximum value from that data and conceiving ways to gather and make business meaning from this new information.

- **Technical "art of the possible" and product roadmaps:** The embedded H3 IT personnel should track the rapid changes in SMAC technologies, and determine which are suited to a specific product or service. They should work closely with product managers to determine which ones become inserted into the product roadmap.

Putting the New IT Organization into Place

The question, though, is how to properly implement this new hybrid model with the H3 organization. We have five recommendations:

1. **Federate H3 IT.** H3 IT resources will mostly sit with the business—an edict you must proclaim within IT as well as with the business units. In our experience, such nonnegotiable pronouncements have been music to the organization's ears; companies usually want the technology capability embedded, or even owned. However, many groups have felt compelled to go their own way without these kinds of commitments from IT. Such declarations create clarity and motivate business resources to work with IT on their Code Halo initiatives rather than "going rogue." We've also found this approach to motivate central IT staff who will self-select to work directly with the business on cool SMAC Stack and Code Halo initiatives.

2. **Jointly fund business unit technology initiatives.** IT should offer to co-fund H3 staff and projects with the business unit on a 50/50 basis and establish joint BU and IT reporting lines. In doing so, these H3 IT leaders will work in full partnership with the business on a daily basis. They will also liaise with central IT to ensure full coordination.

3. **Execute specific projects to drive the transition.** The most effective way to establish business-embedded H3 capabilities is on the back of specific Code Halo, SMAC technology, and

product management projects. The alternative to this approach is simply placing the resources within the business unit without specific project work and hoping for the best. This approach usually fails because IT resources landing in a business unit with no work assigned are often quickly marginalized and abandoned.

4. **Reframe IT's goals.** The goals for H1 and H2 IT, overall, should remain largely unchanged. However, H3 initiatives will usher in a new set of aims for IT. Business-oriented objectives—such as sales, customer engagement, and product-based data generation—should be included along with more technology-based goals such as server uptime, lowering total cost of ownership of technology, and portfolio rationalization.

5. **Assign a mini-CIO to H3.** Because H3 IT competencies are new, you have to tailor them to meet your company's specific needs. Appoint an H3 CIO to orchestrate the people, processes, methodologies, and resources across the business. Though it has become fashionable in some circles to refer to this role as the "Chief Digital Officer," the responsibilities are more similar to those of a classic CIO. He or she is just focused on H3 technologies and initiatives. Establishing this role is important for IT personnel embedded in the business units. Product managers don't want to manage IT career paths, and they don't want to worry about vendor management, development methodologies, or integration with central IT. Find a hybrid manager for this position whose job it will be to focus on the art of the possible with Code Halos, but who is also grounded in the pragmatic realities of your IT legacy.

We have observed in working with customers that some business people struggle to see the potential value of Code Halo opportunities. How can the truck we manufacture take advantage of this idea? How can the supermarkets we run benefit from this approach? In most cases, the root cause of this lack of vision is that business people ultimately responsible for commercial results don't really understand technology—and the people responsible for delivering IT don't fully understand the business. By placing H3 skills into business units and giving both IT and the business unit "skin in the game," your organization will be better aligned to unlock new levels of value.

Create Halo Heroes by Bridging the IT-Business Gap

Merging the physical and the virtual is the management challenge—and opportunity—of our generation as "software eats the world." Organizations that fully integrate business and IT will be able to capitalize on this opportunity. Training your IT and business people to think in this way is the most important challenge that Halo Hero IT leadership must address in order to capitalize on the opportunities in a Code Halo world.

Summary of Part II

Four Principles for Success in the Code Halo Economy

We've seen in Part II how design is becoming central to creating value in an economy of knowledge and insight, and we've explored some of the challenges—and potential solutions—for avoiding evil in an era where transparency and openness is a more common expectation within our personal and professional lives. Professional success in a Code Halo world will require a new set of rules and practices, and we've presented six ideas on how to win in the wirearchy. This new economy will run on technology, so we outlined how you can fine-tune your IT organization to make them Halo Heroes.

In Part III, we'll look in more tactical detail at the Crossroads Model and how to apply it to your organization's challenges and opportunities.

PART III

WINNING WITH THE CROSSROADS MODEL

CHAPTER TWELVE

Seize Advantage During Ionization: Sense, Innovate, and Prepare to Pilot

"If you always do what you always did, then you will always get what you always got."

—Unknown

As we discussed in Chapter 6, we call the first stage of the Crossroads Model "Ionization" because there is an electrified sensation in your organization's environment during this period. The canny business leader is aware that a great new challenge is imminent, an enormous new opportunity is shaping up—but the exact nature of that challenge is as yet unclear.

Based on our research and client work, we know that organizations in a wide range of industries and in markets around the world already know that their business environment is in a state of Ionization. Things feel different, a little strange, and the business-as-usual approach is not producing the results it once did. They know there is a "future of work" ahead that's very different from the current model. Yet many aren't precisely sure about what that means—or where to start.

Your Goal for Ionization Is an Action Plan

Your goal for the Ionization phase, therefore, is to move from the recognition that something **needs** to happen to **making something happen.** Specifically, you want to develop a portfolio of three to six Code Halo ideas ready for pilot.

The following five actions will help you find high-potential pilot ideas within your company and successfully plot a course forward:

1. Prepare your organization for innovation.
2. Map your value chain.
3. Scan your market for signs of Ionization.
4. Listen for new voices in your organization.
5. Pick your Code Halo targets.

Action #1: Prepare Your Organization for Innovation

Politicians, business leaders, educators, and pundits all seem to agree on the importance of innovation. Yet we also know that, especially in tough times, the budget axe falls fastest on investments in the new, the untried, the unproven, the risky. Many voices call out: *We can't afford that right now.*

Research and analysis from the Information Technology Innovation Foundation provides abundant evidence that innovation investment has dropped throughout Western countries over the last few years.[1] Although talk about innovation has increased, many measures— including capital expenditures, start-up rates, the number of IPOs, improvement in innovation capacity, and R&D investment—indicate that spending on it has decreased.

As Richard George, professor at Saint Joseph's University Haub School of Business, puts it: "Companies cannot grow through cost reduction and reengineering alone. Innovation is the key element in providing aggressive top-line growth and for increasing bottom-line results."[2] Similarly, researchers at the University of Brussels have found a strong correlation between commercial success and long-term and consistent levels of funding for R&D and innovation initiatives.[3] We couldn't agree more.

Develop the "Will to Innovate"

We know that industry-changers take action during the volatile Ionization phase, while soon-to-be laggards sit on their hands. More than half the companies on the Fortune 500 today launched during recessions or bear markets.[4]

But taking action is not simple. While many leaders recognize the signs of Ionization, and see challenges and opportunities emerging, they're uncertain about how to begin innovating—especially during uncertain times. It's not a surprise, then, that the default reaction is often to do nothing.

Attending to business as usual and hoping that things will turn out OK are understandable, even rational, responses to volatility. Most managers and senior leaders are time-starved, overcommitted, and more than busy managing the well-established strategies, activities, programs, and technologies that have helped them succeed so far. They are usually well aware of the importance of change in today's business environment and organizations. They may instinctively understand that managing change is a critical element of their work. Still, our human instinct is to *minimize change* or its impact. And while the urge to keep things as they are is natural and the desire for stability seductive, this can lead you into a trap.

Successful innovation during the Ionization phase requires that your people develop the *will* to innovate and your organization aligns around it. To help you move from a mindset of "innovation as concept" to become an "innovation-in-practice" company, act on the following:

- **Dump the clichéd innovation rhetoric.** Most companies talk the innovation game; few play it. To maintain credibility and organizational enthusiasm, don't speak of your innovation initiatives until you *actually implement tangible programs.* Your team should see the new organizational structures, funding initiatives, and personal career opportunities for pursuing innovation. Of course, this is easier said than done; but without such programs, employees will view the posters you put up with slogans such as "Innovation is everybody's job" with derision.

- **Be cheap (and courageous).** We've said that innovation often erupts from environments where costs are low and, therefore, risks are lower, too. When you don't have a fat budget allocation, you are forced to find innovative work-arounds. When you have less risk of losing your fat budget— since you don't have one—your imagination is free to work on the problem itself. Indeed, innovating on a shoestring has a long and storied track record. The most startling innovations rarely originate from individuals or organizations flush with cash, but rather from those who believe most deeply in their work. Steve Wozniak (Apple), Mark Zuckerberg (Facebook), and Marc Benioff (salesforce.com) all famously launched their initial breakthroughs on the cheap.

- **Set goals of .10x and 10x.** Many of the innovative technologies that have emerged in the last few years—including software as a service, social media, and mobile functionality—were created with budgets far smaller than those consumed by previous generations of enterprise technology developers. In fact, we've often seen an inverse relationship between funding and actual innovation. Therefore, be frugal and force your teams to think and act as hungry start-ups. Give them goals of .10x and 10x; that is, their Code Halo solution should cost them 1/10th of the traditional approach, and yet yield 10 times the results. Goals like this help frame the initiative as true innovation vs. incremental improvement.

- **Give time and attention to lean innovation ideas.** Innovation may not need massive financial investment, but it does require nurturing and support. Thus, while you may not be investing a lot of budget, you are investing time, energy, tools, and facilities. Be prepared to arm your disenfranchised, hungry, and introverted individuals and teams—who are perhaps spread in the far corners of the world—with the tools and attitudes to innovate. Provide them with low-cost, pay-as-you-go technology services such as Amazon Web Services, Yammer, and Foursquare. Challenge them to rethink, reinvent, and rewire their organizations, products, and services—indeed, their very

DNA—to create Code Halo-oriented innovation. Ultimately, this means preparing your organization—and yourself—to embrace the "shock of the new," the discomfort of disruption, and the benefits of failure.

- **Think like a venture capitalist and create a culture that accepts failure.** Many VC funds think like pro baseball players; that is, you're an all-star if you hit over .300. Venture capitalists build a portfolio of companies because they know that only a handful will drive positive returns; most of the others will provide middling returns or fail outright. You should take a similar approach as you develop your pilot programs; expect and accept that some will fail. This is a different mindset than many companies are used to taking. It requires fostering a culture that tolerates failure; where you don't punish team members if their pilot fails but instead congratulate them for taking the initiative and risk. Then you encourage them to try again with something else.

- **Commit leadership to your Code Halo initiative.** Nothing says "This initiative is important" as much as putting one of your most successful line managers—one with deep experience and responsibility for a sizable P&L—on the project. When you assign a valuable manager to an innovation initiative, you send the message that being an innovation manager is as important as being a scale manager.

Ionization Is the Time for Entrepreneurs to Shine

Nurturing entrepreneurial thinking is absolutely critical during Ionization. It's a time to encourage your best leaders to look for uncharacteristic events and odd maneuvers that existing competitors or newcomers and upstarts have made. It's when you want your people to stop talking and start doing, to embrace new ideas for products and services, and to take career-defining, game-changing risks. Make it abundantly clear that the "good old times" will never return, but that better, vastly different times await—if you innovate.

You and your team must establish a "no excuses" environment. You won't take "no" for an answer, won't say "we can't do that" because of budget, or timing, or culture, or resources.

Action #2: Map Your Value Chain and Identify Potential Code Halo Connections

Every organization creates some form of value by **converting inputs to outputs.** Michael Porter's 1985 book *Competitive Advantage* introduced rigor into dissecting how this happened so that leaders could create more productive organizations.[5] Mapping your value chain gives you a foundation from which to plan your pilots against your specific organization.

Michael Porter's Value Chain Model

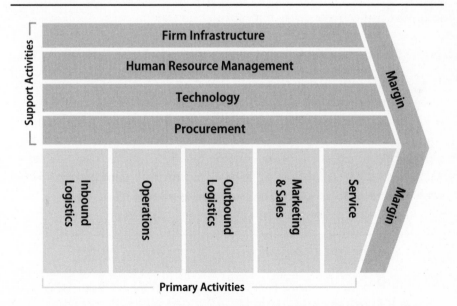

Source: Adapted with the permission of Simon & Schuster Publishing Group from the Free Press edition of COMPETITIVE ADVANTAGE: Creating and Sustaining Superior Performance by Michael E. Porter. Copyright © 1985, 1998 by Michael E. Porter. All rights reserved.

Figure 12.1

We're not going to go into detail about value chain concepts here, but we *are* going to help you connect this concept to Code Halos. (See Figure 12.1 for a version of Michael Porter's Value Chain Model.[6] There are many ways to assess value created in an organization. We think this is one of the most common and effective, and we're assuming it makes sense to you. If not, you should definitely look into Porter's work.)

You don't need to go through a full value chain analysis at this point. You should simply sketch out your organization's value chain to get a high level picture of how your organization works at a rough process level. If it takes longer than a few hours, or you feel like you're drowning in diagrams or slides, you're doing more than you need to in order to get started. Just try to outline the basics of your value and process anatomy.

Once created, you can use this as the foundation for your market scan (described in Action #3), and the value chain becomes a baseline for your transformation since, over time, you can refer to it and use it to assess your performance against competitors. Once you've got a clear picture of your foundation, the next step is to begin to list where new solutions could make sense for your organization.

Identify Connection Points Where Code Halo Solutions Fit

The essential idea during this stage is to look for Code Halo connection points between people, organizations, or devices that fit within your value chain. To find your ideal starting points—those high-impact connections where you can use insight and information to transform a moment of engagement between people, organizations, and devices— it's best to start by looking at your organization's **core process areas such as strategy, product design, or sales and marketing.**

Think about your organization, your value chain, some critical processes where Code Halos can make a difference—and let your creativity flow.

In order to brainstorm a preliminary list of Code Halo ideas, consider each of the processes listed in Figure 12.2, where we've provided a few framing questions to guide you. Think about your organization, your value chain, some critical processes where Code Halos can make a difference—and let your creativity flow. The goal is simply to create a long list of ideas in line with your specific organization.

Brainstorm Your Code Halo Ideas

Process	Food for Thought	Your Code Halo Ideas
Strategy	– How can you improve decision making by sharing information among team members?	
Design	– How can you help connect client input into the design and development of new products and services?	
Manufacturing	– Are there ways to connect devices and/or people to improve your delivery operations? – Are there SMAC Stack solutions that can generate or manage data across your supply chain?	
Selling and Servicing	– How can you use technology to better connect customers to your services and products? – How can you engage new customers with better use of technology?	
Operations	– Can you share code more effectively to improve HR, IT, or procurement?	
Finance	– How can you share data and insight to improve financial management in your organization?	

Figure 12.2

Action #3: Scan Your Market for Signs of Ionization

It's essential to understand what innovative new ideas are emerging in your industry, and to learn from those efforts—those that have both succeeded and failed. This will require you to scan the market to see what Code Halo deployments already exist in your industry, as well as across all industries in the key process areas or product sets on which you are focusing. Look at competitors and start-ups. Read analysts' reports in your sector. Conduct a formal review of venture capitalists and private equity players to figure out where and how they are investing. This is especially critical, because these investors are betting big on the future of Code Halos—and early stage investment is a great clue that a sector is entering the Ionization phase. This digging will help you discover where sparks may already be flying.

The subtle signs will be there today in your market. The question is: Have you built the institutional mechanisms to see and properly read these signs? The scale or "success" of these solutions is irrelevant at this stage of the Crossroads Model. What *is* relevant is **the number of them** and—more important—**where they are appearing.** For example, have other organizations—from start-ups to established competitors—independently created products and services around a certain set of customers or category of products? If so, they may be onto something; after all, how did several independent entities come to the same investment conclusions? For example, multiple airlines are working to create an enriched cabin experience. Uber and Hailo have both appeared in different cities to improve the taxi booking process. Many car companies are exploring how to convert a car into a mobile technology platform. The strongest regret voiced by incumbents in industries that have already reached the Crossroads is that they didn't see the competitive shift sooner.

You don't need to predict which solutions are going to rise to the top, or even which ones are going to *work*. Just find out what's on the market now or soon will be, who's creating these solutions, and what their goals seem to be (see Figure 12.3).

Code Halo Market Scan Worksheet

	What's the Code Halo solution?	Who's doing it?	What's the current or expected impact?
Solution 1			
Solution 2			
Solution 3			
Solution 4			

Figure 12.3

Action #4: Listen for New Voices in Your Organization

If the "usual suspects"—meaning those members of your teams with whom you most often interact—could innovate, they'd have done so already. However, the custodians of the current business model are often not the ones who will drive the new one. This requires you to deliberately seek out, and carefully attend to, the **new voices** in your organization. This isn't just about finding people from lower down in the organization; it's about actively seeking new, challenging mind sets to help drive new ideas.

So where do you find these mind sets? Figure 12.4 has some answers.

Find Innovative Voices In Your Organization

Location of Innovative Voices	Characteristics of Innovative Voices
The Edge	People at the edge are not part of headquarters "group think," not vested in decisions already made, and who have little to lose from saying "no" or "that's a stupid way of doing business." They can be found in: – Distant geographies. – Operating units. – Acquired entities that are not yet fully integrated. – Standalone divisions. – Subcontractors. – Strategic partners. – Advisory firms. – Independent-minded consultancies.
The Bottom	Top-down, "ordered" innovation is rare; organic, bottom-up innovation is chaotic, messy, and unmanageable—which is why those who manage for a living feel so uncomfortable with the process of innovation. However, innovation that emerges from the bottom has an inherently higher probability of producing genuine new insight.

Location of Innovative Voices	Characteristics of Innovative Voices
The New	New employees can bring fresh insights, informed by their experience of how other companies or settings solve those problems. Newly hired managers and executives who have experienced successes and failures elsewhere can act as external change catalysts for as long as 18 to 24 months in their new position. After that, they may fall prey to "that's how we do things around here" thinking.
The Digital	People in younger generations have less commercial experience but plenty of fresh perspective. And if you've hired the right ones, they also possess that most precious of commodities: energy—the ability to hustle, ignore embedded wisdom, and think anew about how things could be better.
The Introverted	Those with the loudest voices frequently win in business— and everywhere else— even if their ideas are the weakest. Introverts (often highly creative and original in their ideas and expression) often lack the desire or the confidence to speak up or force their point in the face of intimidating situations. As a result, they tend to let others dominate and dictate. By seeking the views of the lowest-key person in the room, you can often tap into new seams of un-mined breakthrough thinking.
The Disenfranchised	Sometimes, outside views are lurking in plain view inside the organization. Of course, there are usually good reasons why some people who don't fit within an organization aren't part of the decision-making process. A by-product of this inherent competition is that good people with good ideas can become excluded—disenfranchised, even—from the flow of ideas, discussion, and decisions. When you require original ideas, these somewhat peripheral and "difficult" people (as they're sometimes labeled) have little desire, incentive, or permission to offer their unusual points of view. Naturally, the enfranchised are prone to protect their territories, based on their business-as-usual views.

Figure 12.4

Don't Lock Out New Ideas During Ionization

When we look at companies that have faced their own Extinction Events, everything seems so obvious—in hindsight. "If only Blockbuster had looked at its own data." "If only Kodak had fully embraced digital imagery." "If only Digital Equipment Corporation could have…." Often, these failures were a matter of perspective. That is, when you're harnessed to the conventional cash cow it's difficult to see the new and superior ways of approaching the market.

To avoid this, you have to work assiduously to create a new internal perspective. If you work at Acme, for example, instruct your team: "Create the Acme killer. Put us out of business." Tell them to forget about the past: "Think of this as your first day of work. Don't be afraid to question every decision made by the fools who came before you, even if you're one of them." Create an environment for your teams to do things differently, to create something new.

It's essential to listen to people with whom you may not agree during Ionization. It's difficult, and you still have to be smart about where you pay attention, but it's not impossible. In fact, failing to do so will equal a big miss. The voices inside and outside your organization are waiting to share new ideas. Failing to hear them means that innovation will be trapped, which jeopardizes your company's long-term success—and even survival.

Action #5: Pick Your Code Halo Targets

It's now time to further develop your initial brainstorms and focus on the **art of the possible.** There may be five or six solid ideas worth exploring in your company, so start by identifying the ideas that could deliver real impact. Think first about the problems generating heat at your firm—that you hear about every day:

- "If we could only _____ customers would love us."
- "If we could connect with customers when they are

_____ it would be like we're printing money."

- "We keep getting beat up on social media because we _____
  _____ ."
- "We could achieve our mission more effectively if we could more deeply understand _____ about our services."

Pick Your Code Halo Starting Points

Before entering the *terra incognita* of industry disruption, Code Halo leaders analyze their situation carefully. The first step is to choose a level of analysis: industry, process, or connection point (see Figure 12.5).

Pick Your Code Halo Starting Point

Level of Analysis: Industry, process, or connection point

☐ **Industry**
(Looking at an entire sector; e.g., capital markets, life sciences, property and casualty insurance.) If you are an economist, CEO, member of the board of directors, or academic, you may want to start here.

☐ **Business process**
(Looking at a specific business activity; e.g., new product design, sales, finance and accounting.) If you are a COO, line of business leader, technology leader, or entrepreneur, you'll likely want to start here.

☐ **Moment of engagement** [7]
(Looking at a specific moment of engagement, often in the consumer space; e.g., purchasing something in a retail store, navigating through a theme park, brushing your teeth, controlling your home security system.) These are point solutions within a dedicated process. If you are an entrepreneur—inside or outside a larger company—you may want to start here, but don't overlook the end-to-end process.

Figure 12.5

Consider the following questions:

- How might you **disrupt the entire industry** in which you operate?
- Which discrete, high-value, or knowledge-driven **business processes**—such as new product development or marketing—might you focus on?
- What **moments of engagement** across the value chain—point of sale transactions, driving a car, submitting expense reports—are most relevant?
- And, most important—**what attempts have you already made** to address this market issue, and what can you learn from those?

Some examples of starting points look like this:

- **Windmills operate as a team.** To maximize the output of wind turbine farms, Siemens embeds software in each windmill to facilitate machine-to-machine communication.[8]
- **"Come in for a pit stop now."** A pending service appointment is automatically scheduled when your mechanic alerts your BMW's on-board diagnostics system that a part required is now in the shop and ready to be installed.[9]
- **Supply chains are becoming Code-Halo-enabled.** A full 25,000 companies rely on information connections managed by supply chain technology platform provider GT Nexus to ensure that all kinds of goods—everything from diapers to surf boards—get where they're going as planned.[10]
- **Helping 11,000 Delta pilots arrive on time.** Pilots collaborated with Boeing subsidiary Jeppesen to develop and launch a paperless navigation tool for the iPad—the industry's first interactive mobile en-route app.[11]

Based on our experience with many customers, we see the most likely targets for getting started orient around the customer experience or with information related to devices. You should consider multiple types of code connections, but be sure not to overlook potential solutions around customers and machines.

You should consider multiple types of code connections, but be sure not to overlook potential solutions around customers and machines.

Assess and Rank Your Pilot Ideas

You should be building a list of potential ideas by now, even though you may not have a clear idea of where to place your innovation bets. Pick the best opportunity for a specific moment of engagement within your context. Consider your broad business goals, examine your process anatomy, and imagine what a Code Halo solution could do to drive tangible business results. How strongly do you feel you could derive value by reimagining a given business process? What could you change if you harnessed the power of a new kind of connection with available information?

Don't try to be overly precise, and don't expect complete solutions. Compile a list of 10 to 12 ideas that may be worth exploring further. Prioritize them, but remember—you can't expect that all of them will succeed.

Your goal for reassessing your process anatomy is to help ensure the ideas you Spark are relevant to your organization. While this might seem obvious, we've seen people get a bit lost chasing an idea that looks good but that doesn't match an organization's strategic agenda. So while this step may seem a bit simplistic, detail is required here— because it's important and frequently overlooked. Maintain a focus on the metrics that your senior leadership will care about: cost per claim, fraud recovery rate, lead generation, manufacturing costs, revenue per customer, healthcare plan enrollment, and the like.

Keeping a close connection to your processes and value chain will help maintain relevance to your organization and keep your Spark from fizzling out.

Prepare to Innovate and Pilot During Ionization

Most successful entrepreneurs will admit the same thing after they launch their business: "I had an irrational belief that I was right." (Of course, the unsuccessful ones felt the same way too!) Keeping the faith in your vision for the future is hard and there will be plenty of reasons to stop along the way. Most new initiatives go through several "valleys of despair." There will be times when you and your team are subjected to criticism, even ridicule. You'll experience setbacks—technical, financial, personnel. But what gets teams through those times is that belief—even if it seems irrational at the moment—that they're on the right path.

The highest impact ideas will emerge from friction points in business. This is where code meets code, and leveraging opportunities at this intersection enables businesses to gain real market advantage.

The actions we've outlined are crucial in helping your organization during the Ionization stage of the Crossroads Model. Ionization is all about sensing change, recognizing where Code Halos may emerge, and preparing to launch your own pilots. The highest impact ideas will emerge from friction points in business. This is where code meets code, and leveraging opportunities at this intersection enables businesses to gain real market advantage.

It is the only way to ignite the Spark that defines the next stage of the Crossroads Model.

CHAPTER THIRTEEN

Create a Spark: Pilot Your Best Code Halo Solutions

It is in the next phase of the Crossroads Model—Spark—that game-changing innovations really come to life. This is where ideas start to take shape, as specific pilots include not just a technical proof-of-concept, but also a full review of the business model, market opportunity, and business case. By assessing all of these in the context of a working pilot, your team can get a complete and objective view of the opportunity and assess whether it makes sense to take it to market.

We call this phase of the model "Spark" because just as a small spark—at the right time and with appropriate context—can start a large blaze of innovation, it can also, if not managed properly, quickly fizzle out. In this chapter, we provide an overview of how to find, launch, and manage Code Halo Sparks.

A successful pilot needn't take a lot of time or money; many can be completed within a few weeks. What they *do* require is executive commitment and intense efforts of a cross-functional team comprised of individuals from IT, appropriate business units, finance, and marketing. By employing Agile methodologies, this team should be able to produce a working pilot rapidly. At the end of this process, a larger cross-functional team should conduct a formal review of the pilot to judge its merits and determine if it should move forward.

Your pilots may look different from one another, and focus on any of the five key Code Halo constituencies—customers, employees, partners, products, or your overall organization. They may have an ambitious or narrowly defined scope. Some may have rich interfaces, while others have almost no interface at all. Regardless of the type of solution you choose to pilot, we have noted four actions needed for successful implementation of Code Halo pilots:

1. Embrace "mass personalization."
2. Build Code Halos around the "main character" of your process.
3. Calibrate the Give-to-Get ratio.
4. Pilot and fine-tune the business model.

Let's look at each in detail.

Action #1: Embrace "Mass Personalization"

The term "mass personalization" has historically been an oxymoron; most products and services aren't personalized because the cost of personalization takes them out of the reach of the masses. Roughly a century ago, Henry Ford's great insight was the *standardization* of production. Most all industries followed this approach. Companies sought to standardize core business processes, too—issuing invoices, collecting on receivables, responding to customer post-sale inquiries, making clothes, etc.—in an attempt to reduce costs, error rates, and cycle times. You can see this playing out on the price tags of customized items. We can buy a $500 suit off the rack or spring for a $10,000 bespoke suit from a Savile Row shop.

The Tradeoff Is Broken by Code Halos

Now however, the cost/quality/personalization tradeoff of the physical, widget-based world has been broken in the digital economy. The good news is that the standardization of widgets—by lowering cost—is facilitating the customization of digits—creating more personalized virtual experiences. The fact that information-based products are not constrained by such compromises leads to a central value proposition of Code Halos: **You can provide highly personalized experiences, aligned to largely standardized products and services, to large numbers of customers.** In other words, Code Halos allow for mass personalization of *many* goods and services.

Consider that the incremental cost of a customer's data—however derived—or in selling or servicing their needs virtually is now negligible. Many of us enjoy the benefits of mass personalization through individually tuned experiences with Amazon, Netflix, Google News, Starbucks, Nike, and others. Once we have enjoyed this kind of individual attention and customization, we find it increasingly difficult to fall back into a world of anonymous industrial processes.

Code Halos allow for mass personalization of many goods and services.

Thus, when building your pilots, focusing on the potential for mass personalization is a good place for many organizations to begin Code Halo exploration. When you and your team think through which customers, products, or services would be the best candidates, you quickly confront questions like: "Who will be the focus?" "Which customers, employees, or partners?" "What do we really mean by personalization?" "What exactly will be personalized?" "Where should we do this in our business model, and in what markets?" And, of course, "How do we get started?"

The first and perhaps most important action to take to answer these questions and Spark ideas is to recognize how data and information can help you break some of the traditional constraints of the physical value chain. To begin to tap into that value, you need to start at the process level of your organization.

Action #2: Build Code Halos Around the "Main Character" of Your Process

Once you and your team start focusing on a specific process, you must find its "main character"—the person or thing that anchors its "story." Every business process that matters in your organization has a main character, the person or thing that is acted on from the beginning to the end of a work process. It connects all—or most—of the steps of some elements of the work your organization does. Pandora's main character is the listening consumer. GE Aviation's is the individual airplane engine. In each case, business results are tied to how well or poorly this main character moves through a process.

Using this approach will help your team apply Code Halo thinking to the complexities of process work.

As an example, let's consider a simple healthcare claim as depicted in Figure 13.1. This example presents a very coarse level of granularity simply to illustrate the point without getting into the real-world complexity of your work.

The Process of an Insurable Event

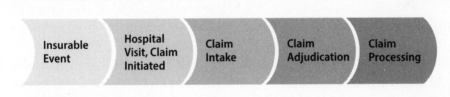

Figure 13.1

- **The insurable event:** You're hit by a car while riding your bike.
- **The hospital visit and claim initiation:** The hospital staff diagnoses a minor leg fracture, puts you in a splint, and sends you hobbling on your way after you hand over your co-payment. The hospital also initiates a claim for reimbursement from your healthcare insurer.
- **Claim intake:** Your insurer takes in the claim, cleans the data, confirms it has the information needed, and validates your coverage.
- **Claim adjudication and processing:** The insurer then adjudicates the claim and decides what to pay based on your coverage. If there are any issues, the claim may be routed to a separate subprocess. The claim then moves into the payment process. Your insurer reimburses the hospital for what it decides to cover.

Most of these steps are manual, labor intensive, and do not benefit much (or at all) from Code Halo thinking. For example, you have little visibility into the whole process, the hospital and insurer are constantly at odds, and the information is often screwed up at the intersect points. It's no surprise that consumer satisfaction levels with insurers are extraordinarily low.[1] A company that could excel in claims work would revolutionize the market.

But who is the main character here? Is it the individual who had the accident? Is it the hospital? Or, is it the claim? In this case, it's *the claim*. If reimagined—with process-level information and insight around the claim—the claim's halo would connect you with the Code Halos around your doctor, the hospital, your insurer, and with your bank. All steps would be orchestrated, with the information halo around the claim continually inflating as it moves through the process.

With the claims-based Code Halo, organizational handoffs would be seamless and error-free. There would no longer be duplication of effort. The hospital would provide individualized care based on your specific needs. The insurer would gain further insight and intelligence on you as the insured, the procedure, and the hospital. And, most important, a patient could focus on his or her *recovery*—not the hassle and irritation of this process.

By focusing on the main character and reimagining how Code Halos could remake this process, the business metrics that healthcare payers care about could be vastly improved. Business outcomes like time (how long the process took), key stakeholder satisfaction (both healthcare providers and plan members), the number of insurable events, overall cost per claim, and how this process can create differentiation in the market would *all* be improved.

Action #3: Calibrate the Give-to-Get Ratio

Another clarifying test for determining the viability of a new initiative is to determine its **Give-to-Get** ratio. We explored this concept in Chapter 9; that is, what one person is willing to give in a commercial transaction versus what they receive in return. This ratio indicates the real value of the connection. To date, consumer market leaders have been thriving as the Give-to-Get ratios in their business models are so significantly in their favor. Customers give very little, and get a lot in return.

However, what happens when the perceived give becomes too much? What happens when it's time to share your financial details, or your medical history, or the location of your children?

Companies have always wanted information about us; after all, we're still being asked for our telephone number or postal code at retail checkouts. But collecting information is far easier—and cheaper—in our virtual economy. We're already inundated with requests for likes, up-votes, loyalty plans, shares, and more. Everyone seemingly wants our code, but if we aren't clear on the value of giving it, these initiatives quickly turn from something we're happy to share to something bothersome and off-putting.

For a solution to Spark you'll need to determine the optimal balance of both giving and getting. All participants in the Code Halo have to see this as a "good deal."

The Hierarchy of Giving and Getting

Our analysis shows there is a clear hierarchy of both giving and getting. The list in Figure 13.2—based on the maturation of consumer-based services and solutions—prioritizes "gives" from easiest to hardest for a consumer. This hierarchy makes it clear that the potential "gets" increase as the "gives" get more difficult. Figure 13.3 lists some of the most important "gets," ranked from most compelling to least compelling.

The Hierarchy of Giving

Type of Code Halo	Examples	The Upside	The Challenges
Entertainment	Pandora, iTunes, Netflix, Amazon, StumbleUpon, YouTube	Music, movies, books, TV shows and blogs. The vast majority of consumers are willing to give information on their tastes.	Negligible downside —this Give passes the "The New York Times front page story" test. That is, most consumers wouldn't care if their personal information in these Gives became public information.
Social	Facebook, Orkut, Google+, Twitter, Match.com, eHarmony, Fotolog	While this Give is a bit higher than information about entertainment choices, hundreds of millions of consumers are, again, more than willing to provide their likes and dislikes, myriad photographs, location, relationship status, and personal opinions.	While such intimate details seem to be a more significant Give, the Get—in terms of human connection—has provided a compelling trade-off.
Consumer	Amazon, eBay, AirBnb, CouchSurfing, Chirpify, Stylehive	This is the tap root of eCommerce. For years, we've given our financial information, data on what we're willing to buy, and what we may be interested in purchasing at some future date. Millions of us vote daily with our wallets and mouse clicks that the convenience and prices make this a worthwhile Give.	This information is still broadly seen as fair game for sharing, but there are trade-offs. There's always some level of risk—though often over-blown—associated with electronic payment, and many feel that their consumer activities are fairly personal. Also, consumers are becoming more selective on these gives— providing them freely on more commodity products, yet being less open on personalized or highly-personal products.

Easiest to Give

Location-Based Services	Waze, Foursquare,	Sharing where you're driving at all times, down to not just the last mile, but the last foot? That's what 50 million users of Waze are willing to provide. Yet, the Give in this market has proven elusive to those unable to (a) generate trust, and (b) provide a Get as clear as "get there as fast as possible," and "don't get pulled over by the cops."	This gets into a zone of discomfort for many who are concerned about having all movements tracked in a database. And while relatively rare, there are examples of people doing bad things based on knowing where you are. The perceived risk raises the level of Give required as well as the level of trust needed before information is shared.
Personal Advice	Thumb	Personal advice is, well, personal. It's usually consigned to the realm of friends … those who know you, and whom you trust. Yet friends aren't experts, and often aren't objective.	Most people are simply not comfortable with the idea of their domestic issues, problems with chemical dependency, depression, etc. being broadly shared. The Give here needs to be significantly valuable to overcome an increasingly high barrier to sharing information.
Career Management	LinkedIn	For many, if it's not on LinkedIn, you didn't really do it. Even if you're not looking for a job, you don't really have a footprint in your company if you're not showing up on LinkedIn. Plus, management now has to recognize that poor behavior is going to be broadly shared.	There's a risk that the current home team now has visibility into your aspirations. Good bosses are fine with people actively managing their careers, but not everybody is a good boss. The downside risk for many organizations is that LinkedIn knows more about your people than the HR department.

The Hierarchy of Giving

Type of Code Halo	Examples	The Upside	The Challenges
Financial	Google Tip Jar, eTrade, Mint	If you're online, chances are you are exchanging your financial code. These processes have had time to harden, and are now seen as highly secure. The upside— transparency, availability to actively manage our money, easier transactions, etc. —are now a part of our normal fiscal lives.	Most investment agencies and banks have terrific protection against actual theft against individuals. Even so, having your financial information become public would—for most—feel like a huge invasion of privacy.
Medical	WebMD, DailyStrength, LoseIt!, Traineo	Consumers have proven willing to give relatively innocuous "improvement-based" personal medical information, such as improving their workouts, losing weight, better medical management, etc.	Medical and legal personal information is generally highly regulated—and we may not be willing to share this information with anyone. Imagine your AIDS or cancer diagnosis being accessible to a potential employer—or romantic date. The downside could be life-altering, so we only share this when there is the highest degree of trust.

Hardest to Give

Figure 13.2

The Hierarchy of Getting

Type of Code Halo	Examples	The Upside	The Challenges
Customized/ Curated Experiences	Netflix, Amazon, Pandora, Disney's MagicBand	The "wow" factor, and subsequent emotional connection, that's established when we're able to collaborate with others to get more personalized experiences in dining, movies, books, travel, etc.	Potential for "narrowcasting" and "echo chamber syndrome" of not being exposed to new ideas, concepts, forms of art and entertainment, etc. There's a real potential for the loss of serendipity.
Personal Relevance and Human Connection	Facebook, Twitter, Orkut, Google+	Enhancement of personal relationships, being "kept in the loop," one-to-one connection with friends, family, and even strangers, and a heightened sense of personal relevance.	Facebook depression syndrome: The sense of inadequacy and increased loneliness that comes from viewing the curated and idealized views of others' lives. Equating online relationships with real human connections.
Time and Convenience	Waze, Yelp, TripAdvisor	It's night. The car breaks down, so you're on the roadside, and you'll never make it to your hotel. Using your mobile devices, what would have meant sleeping in your car or a risky hike now results in a tow truck, new hotel reservation, and hot dinner.	Concerns are growing about having others know our location. Also that easy answers mean eroded problem-solving skills for the highly digital literate.

Most Compelling Get

The Hierarchy of Getting (continued)

Type of Code Halo	Examples	The Upside	The Challenges
Cost Savings, Price/ Performance	eBay, Priceline, GE Brilliant Machines	Price transparency has already led to new models of conducting business for physical products. New commercial models—auctions, as-a-service pricing, etc.—have also become more common.	As price competition decreases, more things become commodities. But not all products are like oil or soybeans. They need investment, innovation, future development. There's a risk that complete price transparency continues to trim margins. This is good for near-term cost savings, but it might have a chilling effect on new development and customer services.
Personal Improvement, Self-Actualization	LoseIt!, Nike+ FuelBand, Garmin Connect	Whether it's losing weight, or completing a triathlon, having a support group can help maintain momentum toward improvement.	You probably wouldn't tell your boss how many pounds overweight you are. Some of this information is considered intensely personal—and those deemed "unfit" may end up without affordable healthcare coverage.
Money	Progressive Insurance's Snapshot	Who doesn't like money? In the right places—such as Progressive's Snapshot—it appeals to a subset of customers.	Who doesn't like money? One who has come for something different. Money actually cheapens the experience when other attributes are expected. Money—in many cases—baldly states, "We are providing you with no other value. This is all about us."

Least Compelling Get

Figure 13.3

Pick Your Code Halo Based on Its Give-to-Get Ratio

Figure 13.4 provides a model that can be used during the Spark phase to help choose where to invest your innovation time and capital. Sort your initial long list of potential Spark pilots into the following three categories in your preliminary triage of ideas.

Initial Give-to-Get Assessment Model

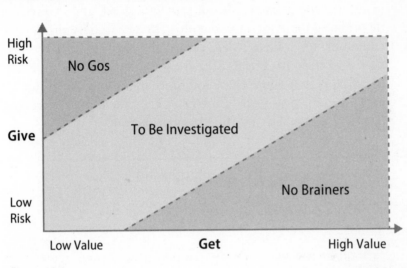

Figure 13.4

1. **No Go:** These ideas have a high-risk "give" and a meaningless "get" for people or organizations. If you want an organization's compliance records or a person's genome, but aren't delivering significant value in return, then forget it and move on to another idea more likely to Spark.

2. **To Be Investigated:** Most of your ideas will land here. It won't be clear whether the Give-to-Get ratio works at this point; unfortunately, that's the price of innovation. But that means it's time to explore, to test some assumptions with a test group, to dig more deeply into technologies. An early investigation here—or even a simple pilot—can be inexpensive

and immensely useful in helping set an investment direction. Real competitive differentiation will often come from these solutions.

3. **No Brainers:** In most sectors, there are some clear Code Halo investments you must quickly embrace to avoid competitive disadvantage. Imagine, for example, an auto company that in five years does not produce cars that connect drivers and passengers to a more enriched driving experience. Or, an insurance company that is not protecting cash and investment by utilizing more member data to refine its underwriting equations. Or, a life sciences company not using information to de-risk clinical field trials. These companies will be significantly handicapped, because these solutions are a "must have" for organizations over time. They may seem like innovations now, but they will rapidly become hygiene factors.

Code Halos are not just a new technology; they are the new business.

Let's look at a travel example. Building customer-focused Code Halos for the in-flight experience is a "no brainer" for airlines. A "social cabin" solution would allow flyers to share information on their entertainment, food, and travel preferences. With such information, the airline could (for a modest fee) turn what can sometimes feel like a five-hour hostage siege into a highly personalized entertainment and culinary experience.

Such a solution would transform an airline's role from being a mere carrier to an orchestrator of an integrated end-to-end experience. A "social cabin" would allow an airline to turn an often negative experience into a positive one full of connection and enjoyment.

What else could airlines be investigating beyond what goes on aboard the aircraft? Imagine an experience that extends to the whole travel process—before, during, and after a trip. As the most complicated

A "social cabin" would allow an airline to turn an often negative experience into a positive one full of connection and enjoyment.

and expensive part of most journeys, the airline could use a Code Halo philosophy to provide value (gives) from the moment you book a trip to the time you arrive home. It could reinvent the booking process, link more effectively to hotels, and integrate with financial institutions and others to help manage other aspects of a trip such as securing transportation or booking events or locating resources. Rather than focusing only on flight, it could expand its offering to cover the entire experience of moving from point A to point B—in the most beautiful way possible.

Action #4: Pilot and Fine-Tune the Business Model

Code Halos are not just a new technology; they are the *new business*. To that end, your Spark pilot cannot simply be a technical proof-of-concept. It must also be a business proof-of-concept. Therefore, the Spark pilot teams should outline the new business model you're presenting in conjunction with the technical pilot. As such, the team must consider:

- **The new process flow:** It's vitally important to recognize the virtual processes that will operate in combination with existing physical processes. The team needs to get granular and tactical to decompose and restructure the new business process. It must understand how the refined process operates, what the key components are, and what will be easy and difficult to implement.

- **Conflicts with the old:** Your team can develop tunnel vision in the rush to build the new and lose sight of potential conflicts with your existing business. At the advent of eCommerce, Dell Computer was gobbling up market share with its Internet-based, direct-to-market model. Then, Compaq Computer fully diagnosed Dell's eCommerce model and—from a technical perspective—successfully replicated and neutralized it. However, Compaq's eCommerce system was in direct conflict with its established direct sales force—and as such, was crushed by *internal* resources. Thus, your team should be clear-eyed about potential conflicts and unintended negative consequences on your Code Halo initiative during the Spark pilot.

- **The business case:** You need to outline the costs of the Code Halo solution implementation and full business model, along with the anticipated revenue and reputational gains. We've found it difficult to fully determine the latter with many Code Halos, as they have the ability to scale so quickly. Thus, the team should focus on ranges based on conservative assumptions.

- **Fit with your current organizational culture:** Initially, this may seem to be an esoteric question about the "soft" stuff. However, many stakeholders state that these are the very issues that prove the most difficult to overcome in looking back after an implementation. Therefore, you need to think about your organization's cultural attributes, how things "really" get done, and ask: Is the proposed Code Halo in alignment or conflict with such cultural norms?

- **The ecosystem:** Code Halos often require you to work with your business partners to see new correlations in your data and recognize new mutual sales opportunities. A customer's moment of engagement will likely cut across several different companies (or even industries). The customer insight in our previous airline example is not just gleaned from how a passenger behaves on the plane; carriers can gather additional information through understanding what kinds of hotels they prefer, what type of car they rent, and other activities and behaviors. Car manufacturers are actively seeking ways to share—and gain access to—data with ecosystem partners to create new information-based offerings and services.

The Spark Is the Healthy Beginning, Not the End

All the activities in the Spark phase should help you pick your pilot initiatives and go. However, igniting Sparks is not easy. The challenge every enterprise faces is to find the *right* Spark among the countless ideas that are floating around among its atomic business processes. You will know something big is happening when:

- Process-aligned Code Halos—sharply focused on the proper main character—meet algorithms.
- Virtuous Give-to-Get ratios emerge.
- New business models take form as unique value propositions.
- Scaling begins, as both the number of users and usage begin to grow virally.

When these things happen, it's a signal to move on to the next phase of the Crossroads Model. It's not enough to build an interaction platform. At this point you're now competing with a new set of rules, and for your Code Halo-based solutions to succeed you (and they) must move through a rigorous learning process. You must augment solutions and products by meaning derived from a steady stream of data and information. We call this next stage **Enrichment.**

CHAPTER FOURTEEN

Enrich and Scale at Internet Speed: Turn a Spark into a Blaze

Little may appear to happen after you launch your pilots in the Spark phase, at least in terms of traditional business metrics. This period of Code Halo build-out often creates tension for leaders who are betting on a telematics device, a crowdsourced product design, or a mobile app. Entrepreneurs will be sitting on pins and needles hoping it will scale like a virus.

However, these are the wrong considerations at this phase—because a lot is happening that traditional metrics might not show. The organization learns during Enrichment, and algorithms get smart based on meaning derived from business analytics. You refine and improve the initial Code Halo to fit the specific needs of your customers and market. You will enter the Enrichment phase with a nascent Code Halo initiative, yet—if successful—exit this phase with a rapidly growing, robust, and potentially game-changing solution.

You want to look at Enrichment as a **greenhouse phase** that allows the new business model to grow in a healthy way. As such, the early parts of this stage require patience. Managers who focus too early on "moving the needle" in traditional business metrics can actually do great damage—if not stop the Enrichment process altogether.

Central to this success is filling your Code Halo with data. Your team should be obsessed with the ongoing accumulation of the right data during Enrichment, but also recognize that this accumulation is only a means to an end. After all, we named this phase "Enrichment" because the raw materials of data need to be *enriched*—enhanced and augmented when your business analytics convert mountains of ones and zeros into real business value. As such, Big Data is not about the mountain of data; it's about getting "big answers."

Think of how iTunes grew slowly from 2004 to 2007, creating a foundation for massive growth later on (10 billion songs downloaded in 2010, exploding to 20 billion songs only 18 months later).[1] Facebook followed a similar pattern by taking several years to get to 100 million users in 2008, but then adding another 100 million users on average every 167 days until it reached 1 billion users late in 2012.[2] Along the way, these sites focused on user experiences and information generation. Once they had these platforms in place, the profit-generating business model began to emerge over time.

Apple and Facebook were ultimately vindicated by so many voting with their fingers. But the business results were not yet obvious in the early days of Enrichment.

Stay the Course Through the Flat Water of Enrichment

Your Code Halo initiative may have an internal PR problem during this phase. During the Enrichment phase, everyone needs to understand the sequencing in play, and realize that there are no shortcuts around the fact that initially lots will be going into the Code Halo initiative—time, money, attention—without much seemingly coming out. There are two issues in particular to recognize and manage:

1. **Information before profits:** Make no mistake, this sequencing is going to create internal dissonance. Certain voices, most likely emanating from the CFO's office, will demand that the new solution needs to start generating revenue and profitability *pronto*. However, asking for bottom-line financial results at this phase of the Code Halo's evolution is like asking an 11-year-old to pick up the tab for dinner. The vast majority of successful Code Halo implementations first had to steer through the flat water of Enrichment, when companies must achieve Code Halo goals—such as a proven online connection with customers, compelling amplifiers and interfaces, data growth, algorithm refinement, and a refined Give-to-Get ratio—before meeting

traditional financial goals. Managing through this period requires leadership and nerves of steel.

2. **The information and platform Catch-22:** You will encounter another dilemma at this stage of the Crossroads Model: you need more users to get more data to enrich the Code Halo, but you need enriched data to attract more users. Solving this Catch-22 is complex and, as with any new endeavor, the odds of success may seem stacked against you. However, there are some actions we have outlined below that can help to ensure your organization succeeds during the Enrichment phase.

Action #1: Ensure a Balanced Focus on All Five Elements of Your Code Halo's Anatomy

As we saw in Chapter 4, which focused on the anatomy of a solution, a successful Code Halo has five core elements: the amplifier, the application interface, algorithms, Big Data, and a commercial model. You will need to develop all five in parallel during Enrichment.

However, we have seen that such a balanced approach is difficult to implement in practice once a team feels the pressure to deliver results. We've witnessed too many teams focus on one or two components of the Code Halo's anatomy at the expense of the others—usually leading to the failure of the overall initiative (such as Microsoft's Zune and Barnes & Noble's Nook). Thus, it is important to ensure that you have included all the elements of a healthy solution.

By using the table in Figure 14.1, you can assess the strength of each attribute of your own solution anatomy. The goal of this simple exercise is not necessarily to attain a high degree of precision, but just a general sense of the overall health of a particular solution. If you feel that something is not working right, come back to this diagnostic to see if you are missing any of the major solution elements.

Code Halo Anatomy Assessment Model

Anatomy Element	Description	Score	Scale
Amplifier (Device)	Any device considered part of the "Internet of Things" (mobile phones, tablets, telematics devices, magic bands, IP-enabled appliances, the powered pill, wearable devices, game consoles).		**5** = The solution is tightly aligned to a mature, effective device (either proprietary or in common usage; e.g., a mobile phone or tablet). **3** = A device or sensor technology is in place, but not as mature; may not be in common usage and have barriers to distribution or use. **1** = The solution is not tied to a functioning device.
Application Interface	This is the intersection point of the user experience. Without this, nothing else matters. It's through this interface that the effectiveness—and the meaning-making—of the Code Halo are displayed.		**5** = The user/customer interface is clean, elegant, intuitive, and beautiful. It causes virtually no barrier to usage; in fact, it even invites usage. User experience design is clearly at the center of the strategy. **3** = The interface is functional, but not particularly intuitive. The form factor may be limited or somewhat weak. **1** = The user interface resembles an out-of-the-box expense system. There is little evidence of a well-constructed, end-to-end user experience design.
Algorithms and Meaning Making	Business meaning has to be drawn from imagination being applied to data captured and de-coded by algorithms. Imagination + Big and Small Data/Algorithm = Business Insight.		**5** = Algorithms are in place and well integrated with human judgment and analysis. The data is not only collected, but the service/product/experience improves as learning is gleaned and applied. **3** = Data is collected, but much of it lies fallow, not contributing to an improved experience or business model. Analytics may be seen primarily as a technology activity, rather than a critical step in the value chain. **1** = There are lots of spreadsheets and perhaps some Herculean efforts, but little impact on the service or experience. Few critical insights are generated—and are not likely to be.

Code Halo Anatomy Assessment Model (continued)

Anatomy Element	Description	Score	Scale
Data	The raw materials for analysis and meaning-making. Without good data, you're really still guessing.		**5** = The solution is collecting data critical to competing based on insight. The data input is mostly "signal" that allows solution builders and managers to fail fast and learn. There is very little noise, and the Code Halo can inflate. **3** = Data is entering, but it's a mix of noise and meaningful business signal. Some decisions are supported, but there are many more questions than answers. **1** = The data input is mostly noise with very little solid business signal. There's not much here to help inflate a Code Halo.
New Business Model	There needs to be a way to monetize the meaning (e.g., Allstate's new commercial model connected to the telematics device; Google ad placement).		**5** = The Code Halo innovation is tightly aligned with an innovative commercial model. This could be price or cost connected to something new or flexible enough to create pricing elasticity. The commercial model should be founded on code and information that drives daily use and personalization, and is in close alignment with a target demographic. **3** = The innovation is accompanied by a business model with some tweaks and partial alignment with usage, but it lacks overall innovation. The business metrics are only somewhat aligned with competition on information and meaning. **1** = The Code Halo solution does not have a corresponding innovative commercial model. The price remains aligned more to a purely physical supply chain. The value of code is not monetized.

Figure 14.1

By presenting the results of this exercise via a spider diagram, for example, you can generate a clear view of the strengths of the solution, and where work is needed. You can create this diagnostic for your own solution, and also for competitive alternatives in the market or best-in-class Code Halos that your team admires. Such scoring provides both objectivity as well as motivational targets.

Action #2: Get the Two Key Pillars Right—The User Experience and the Data

While all five elements outlined earlier are important, two stand out as particularly key—the **user experience** and the **right data sets.** Without these two, nothing else will come together.

Constantly Refine the User Experience

Typically, the initial user experience will be far from perfect. The key at this stage of the model is to apply Minimum Viable Product and Lean Start-Up thinking to determine what will truly engage your users. In assessing what's working—and what's not working—conduct focus groups, review user data in detail, and, if your budget stretches to it, have an outside design agency review your team's work.

Also, remember "user experience" goes well beyond aesthetics. You need to determine whether the experience has "stickiness"; that people utilize it more and more often. Cause and effect will start to become clear when you start reviewing customer acquisition data. You and your team will start to see your solution through your users' eyes. You'll develop an understanding of what's compelling about their experience in your halo, and what you need to improve or discontinue.

Marc Benioff—founder and CEO of Salesforce.com, the leader of the SaaS and cloud revolution—saw the importance of this kind of assessment early on by studying many of the moves Amazon was making. He took inspiration from Amazon's one-click ordering, the aesthetic of the interface, the simplicity of design, and its approach to pricing and economics. These elements are all examples of Amazon tactics that Benioff baked into the Salesforce.com solution with incredible results.

Scale Your Data First, Not Your Business

"What we want in Enrichment is data." You should put that statement on the program status report every day. Whether the data is from machines or people, the goal here is to collect information to *enrich the solution*. You may still want to ask, "What did we earn today?" but you should place the priority on answering the question, "What did we *learn* today?"

Unless you are in a start-up, the toughest part of Enrichment is that what you'll be doing in your organization will be out of sync with what everybody else is doing. They'll be up late closing deals, working the shop floor, managing problems and escalations. You'll be up all night worried about the data you hope will come in.

This is exactly why you must be clear and committed to the near-term goals for your solution. Doing this will improve your chances of moving forward through the Enrichment phase.

Action #3: Use "Metrics That Matter" to Know That the Code Halo Is Inflating

To keep that clear focus and commitment, it's vital during the early stages of Enrichment to establish the Code Halo "metrics that matter" that show progress and allow you to make necessary course corrections. Identifying and isolating those metrics is a difficult process for any startup; without any signposts of success, the blade phase of the hockey stick model of development can be nerve-racking and cause you to feel like you're driving blind. At 110 mph. At night … in fog.

Each individual solution will have its own unique metrics, but here are six general metrics we've seen companies use successfully:

1. **Total number of users:** Although it's a coarse number, that you'll need to refine over time, the overall total number of users is one of the most important signs of traction during Enrichment. Note that for machine-to-machine or app-to-app connections, the user may be a device or software—not necessarily a person. In reviewing the number of users—and the daily growth velocity—you can quickly assess if you have passed the "brochure test," in which the value proposition is compelling enough for somebody to sign up in the first place.

2. **Volume of data:** This should be both transaction data and metadata. You must recognize that metadata—what functionality users browsed, what they liked, what shelf display they looked at, what they ignored—is equally important, maybe more so, than transaction data—e.g., volume of goods/services sold, home address, store location of sale, etc. You should design your solution to capture as much of this metadata as possible.

3. **User engagement:** Knowing how much time users are spending with the Code Halo, what elements they're using, and exactly what they're doing is vitally important. API traffic analysis can give you important clues as to what users like and don't like about your Code Halo and how to develop user interfaces, displays, and workflows to improve your overall value proposition.

4. **Repeat visitors:** A corollary of user engagement, data about repeat visitors, will give you a sense of how sticky your solution is and how much churn surrounds it. Repeat visitors typically are your best advocates and drive significant growth.

5. **Revenues:** You must capture what revenue contribution the Code Halo solution is making, either directly or indirectly, as early in its development as possible.

6. **Total cost of acquisition:** As we've discussed, it can be detrimental to let CFO metrics determine your course in the early stages of development. However, it is important that you measure progress in some ways that accountants can understand. Many start-ups use total cost of acquisition (TCA) to

analyze how much it is costing them to get traction. While the metrics described above should be heading north, this one should head south as quickly as possible; dividing your total "burn rate" by the number of users you are bringing on board introduces a necessary dose of reality into business development discussions.

You must recognize that metadata—what functionality users browsed, what they liked, what shelf display they looked at, what they ignored—is equally important, maybe more so, than transaction data.

Initially, you should collect and be able to report all of these data types on a monthly, weekly, daily, and sometimes even hourly basis. You can then calibrate what frequency is most appropriate over time.

Though there are no hard and fast rules about what rates of growth you should achieve for these metrics, venture capital norms show that monthly growth in the early stages of a new solution should be in the range of 30%–40%, and yearly growth should be over 150%. Facebook grew revenues 188% in 2007, 87% in 2008, 177% in 2009, 158% in 2010, and 114% in 2012.[3] Twitter's user growth (measured by number of Tweets) also showed similar patterns; there were 400,000 Tweets in the first quarter of 2007; 100 million a year later; 50 million a day by February 2010; and 400 million Tweets a day by September 2013.[4] The Nike+ FuelBand sold out online in four minutes in its first run, and was soon being resold for double its retail price on eBay.[5]

Of course, the metrics of these smash hits are the exception not the norm. However, their growth illustrates the nature of the exponential growth curve that your solution will need to achieve to move beyond the pilot phase. Hitting stretch target metrics like these needs to be part of every team member's personal objectives.

It's vital to recognize that the precise nature of the metrics will be volatile and plastic; you may realize that you are measuring the wrong thing, and collecting data that's pointing you in the wrong direction. As noted previously, course correction is inherent at this stage of the model.

Action #4: Capture Code and Make Meaning (But Walk Before You Run)

During Enrichment, the process of turning data into insight should begin to develop its own form of perpetual motion. The learning process becomes self-reinforcing; that is, the more the software learns about the data it analyzes, the more it knows about similar data the next time it sees it. Though we remain a long way away from the Singularity— that theoretical point in time when artificial intelligence surpasses human intelligence—the trajectory of software's education is such that exponential outcomes are bound to emerge from enriched and inflated Code Halos.[6]

Code Halo connections may seem quite crude and simplistic (particularly to consumers) during early Enrichment. You must not be discouraged by this and accept that you have to walk before you can run. Examples that are initially simple, yet open up Code Halo opportunities, include: the Samsung smart fridge, which uses Evernote to keep your shopping list up to date; United Healthcare, which provides information about health and wellness options; and the next-generation smart dispensing machine from both Coca-Cola and PepsiCo.

While you're learning to walk well, you can carry on imagining your solution's possibilities. As it develops and the code base deepens, it can become more sophisticated and functionally rich. In time, we can imagine that the smart fridge will communicate directly with the supermarket, order items, pay, and schedule delivery times synced automatically with your calendar. UnitedHealthcare's Code Halo will provide a health platform that contains historical health records and real-time diagnostics that your sensor-enabled AiQ Smart Clothing will capture. As such, it will deliver heart rate, respiration, skin temperature, and (potentially) EKG results to your primary care physician or an appropriate specialist.[7] Next-generation Coke machines will recognize you and have your beverage of choice ready without you having to touch a single button.

Keep in mind then that although your team may recognize many potentially exotic and exciting conclusions based on the extrapolation of your data, it's best to keep things simple at first. First crawl, then walk, then run. Focus initially on looking for simpler, lower-order insights that early stage ideas will generate. If these are taking hold, their power will be quite evident and their commercial impact will begin to become more material.

Action #5: Be Open to Unanticipated Consequences ... and Success!

There is a rich history of technological innovations that their inventors imagined for use in one context—but that ended up being valuable in some other context altogether. Alexander Graham Bell saw his telephone as a good way of piping music from one room to another. The Internet was envisioned as a military network that could withstand an atom bomb. And Twitter creator Jack Dorsey never imagined that his railroad and taxi scheduling inspired software would end up toppling dictators.[8] Your new idea may have a similar unpredictable fate. If your Code Halo is genuinely inflating and genuinely powerful, then it is highly likely to be doing so in ways that may not be quite what you were predicting or hoping for—but that *work,* nonetheless.

These issues prompt another set of considerations: How do you pursue this unexpected new route and the new options it's opening? Are you even aware of what they might *be*? It would be easy at this stage of the Crossroads Model to be anxious about what you may have unleashed. And this anxiety could make it easy to decide that this is not a route you want to explore. While this is understandable, it is a mistake.

In our analysis of organizations that are starting to succeed with Code Halos, one common thread is that innovators keep an open mind about unintended consequences. As you begin to scale your solution, you'll recognize that new commercial models, new ways to interact with customers, new uses for existing devices, and new customer sets are all "fair game" for successful innovators. The lesson here is that during Enrichment—when your solution touches the real world, and things get a little tougher—you need to nurture and explore new ways of mining and managing code to deliver value.

Action #6: Don't Overlook Change Management

One last aspect of this phase of the Crossroads Model is to focus on managing the change these ideas will introduce. Leaders like you may feel ambivalent toward change management. It's not the sexiest part of developing new ideas. However, it's vital to recognize the role change management plays in making innovation stick.

The good news is that while the Code Halo is a new phenomenon, managing change is as old as the hills. The literature on the topic is broad and deep.[9] We're not going to reprise that here, but there are some tactical points you should familiarize yourself with. The following four approaches will help embed the role of change management into your initiatives:

1. **Leverage professional change management expertise.** Don't fall into the trap of thinking that change management is a pseudomanagement science that you can ignore. High-quality change management is vital to syncing up new ideas and approaches with people, teams, and organizations. It's never easy to *truly* change an existing organization. The wise won't skimp on calling the experts in.

2. **Create internal Code Halo change champions.** As well as hiring outside expertise, nominate a subset of your team to become internal "champions" of the new ideas/initiatives

you are deploying. Focus on making these people your Code Halo advocates and equip them with the knowledge and communication skills to help other members of their team assimilate. Tie elements of their annual review to success here. Highlight and recognize the transitions they have made, and make them central to celebrating subsequent follow-on transitions that other team members make.

3. **Budget for change.** Successful transformation doesn't happen by accident. It is illogical to spend big money on becoming a Code Halo organization only for this to fail because you didn't invest sufficient time or funds on embedding and institutionalizing the change required. This is a common mistake. Be smart by focusing on the line item in your budget spreadsheet that shows how seriously you take the role of change management. The cost may not even be that high, but it's important to include this.

4. **Take field trips.** See the art of the possible by investigating and visiting others who have successful Code Halos in the market. Spend time with them, and have them share their experiences—both good and bad—in getting their initiative from Spark through Enrichment. Discuss challenges in getting their solution to work in harmony with the more established parts of their organization. Find out how they got their senior management teams to learn the disciplines and metrics of managing information. Your team members won't just gain helpful advice and best practices; they'll also develop a renewed sense of purpose and energy to see the solution to maturity.

The cultural issues at the heart of change management—the unspoken norms around admired behaviors, desirable attitudes, Machiavellian politicking—are hard to capture, characterize, and interpret, let alone correct. They are, though, all factors that leaders need to master and be sufficiently skilled in to create the conditions in which Code Halos can flourish.

Enrich Your Solution to Win at the Crossroads

In some ways, Enrichment is the most difficult phase of the Crossroads Model. You will experience several "valleys of despair" and will often have to coach your team—and your organization, and sometimes even *yourself*—to maintain belief in the absence of much tangible evidence. Yet you cannot bypass this phase. Consider that many companies stagnating in the market certainly had enough data to understand they were in the middle of Ionization, but seemingly could not do anything about it. Even with attempts to manage through such change, they erred severely by skipping or short-circuiting the Spark and Enrichment phases—because they failed to understand the nuances of new business models in the context of their specific organizations and markets. Only by experiencing and working through the challenges of these phases can you develop a Code Halo that is truly a catalyst for your business.

Consider your enrichment activities to be analogous to sailing a ship. While a sailor may have a destination in mind, she knows that she usually can't steer the boat directly to that destination. The journey will be a series of tacks and jibes, heading to port, then starboard, then port again, constantly adjusting for wind and tide, continuously rigging and rerigging as conditions dictate. Getting the Code Halo to inflate requires similar skill, patience, and attention. Solutions will almost never inflate on their own. The code you capture from users will continually tell you whether you need to tack or jibe, to go faster or go slower. This feedback loop is one of the defining characteristics of the Internet generation, and smart software and services companies have become highly sensitized and attuned to this message. For your organization, building and managing a solution is not a one-time "set it and forget it" activity. If you're doing things right, the pilot you build in Spark will be quite different from the product or service you designed several months earlier.

CONCLUSION

Winning in the New Code Rush

We are living in a special economic time. A generation from now, we will look back and see that the 2010s was the decade in which commerce changed. We'll see that traditional factors of production and wealth creation—capital, labor, and raw materials—were superseded by digital means of production: SMAC technologies coupled with massive amounts of data. It will be clear that this was the decade in which the digital lives of people, things, and organizations took shape—when the virtual took primacy over the physical. Code Halos are already beginning to create an entirely new economy, full of opportunities of unprecedented scale and possibility.

This transition has profound implications for individuals, businesses of all sizes, and public sector organizations:

- At a personal level, all of us will reform how we interact with all kinds of organizations (and each other). We will reset our expectations about what freedoms and protections we will demand from our governments and regulatory agencies. We will work to strike a new balance between what we can gain in this new world—conveniences, enriched experiences, new insights—and what we might lose, such as personal privacy.

- Large corporations will need to move quickly to meet new market expectations. Customers and investors will increasingly place value on digital offerings and capabilities. In capturing the opportunity of wrapping people, products, and processes with digits, many will have to re-architect portions of their operations and how they engage with customers. Leaders will have to learn new skills such as managing by empiricism, how to more fully integrate technology into business processes, and how to generate mass personalization of products and services.

- Smaller businesses that get it right have the opportunity to become giant-killers. The Trillion-Dollar Club has taught us that innovators can move with unprecedented velocity because digits scale faster than widgets. Without the large capital requirements that are traditional barriers to entrepreneurs, small businesses can embrace cloud-based social tools and low-cost data sets to recode the customer experience. Many elements of business have already been moved to a virtual model, but many transactions will stay local. Local retailers and small businesses are already beginning to use technology and Code Halo ideas to create stronger relationships with customers.

- To meet mission and service goals, governments and public sector organizations can similarly drive new levels of innovation, efficiency, and transparency with Code Halo thinking. Public sector leaders must also quickly strike a new balance where: (a) trust is established with citizens and corporations; (b) legal and tax systems adapt to facilitate, instead of quash, innovation; and (c) protections remain in place to ensure virtual markets remain fair, safe, and transparent.

Similar to previous economic transitions, this new economic model will develop in an unevenly distributed manner. There will be distinct winners and losers—at personal, corporate, industry, and societal levels. Our intention in writing this book is to make that transition more evenly distributed. Prior economic transitions were based more on serendipitous factors such as raw materials, geography, and historical circumstance, but this shift—powered by low-cost SMAC Stack technologies—provides opportunities available to all of us.

The key to success—as we have outlined within this book—is to first recognize the contours of the transition and then follow the proper process to address it. The transitions to date in music, movies, books, phones, and information services serve as our canaries in the coal mine. They have shown a pattern—the Crossroads Model—that we believe will repeat itself again and again in the coming years.

There Are Some Clear Rules for Winning at the Crossroads

In our daily work with clients across many industries in many parts of the world, the Crossroads Model continues to gain more validation nearly every day. Embracing this shift is not something that can be ignored or delayed, and seizing this opportunity requires adopting several new operating principles:

- **Make design central to your value proposition.** Winners will not only provide technical utility and quality, but they will also deliver beautiful digital products and experiences. We really should not be surprised by this for, after all, more traditional sectors—such as automobiles, housing, clothing, and consumer electronics—have long had design as a central factor of success. Similarly, in Code Halo initiatives, delivering beautiful products and experiences has now become mandatory.

- **Don't be evil 2.0.** With great insight comes great responsibility. While Code Halos provide massive economic opportunity, the misuse or mismanagement of customer, employee, and partner information has downsides that could be catastrophic. In the coming years, we will certainly hear of more abuses of privacy and trust as the virtual economy continues its rapid expansion. Ensure your organization has the proper technical, process, legal, and cultural safeguards in place to be seen as a paragon of trust.

- **Manage your career based on code.** Just as the fortunes of products and corporations are changing with Code Halos, so are those of individuals. Some will harness this transition, others will not. Some portions of the management process will remain inviolate, while others will change radically. In the coming few years, be open to the change, embracing what works for you, your employer, and your industry.

- **Make IT your Halo Heroes.** The reports of the death of corporate IT have been greatly exaggerated. In this time of rapidly increasing digitization, corporate IT will become increasingly strategic and central to operations. Yet, this transition will only be successful by moving to a new organizational model that protects prior investments and capabilities while embracing new SMAC-based delivery and organizational models.

- **Create Code Halo solutions in line with the Crossroads Model.** Recognizing and understanding Code Halos is only half of the game. The other half is employing the right set of actions at the right time and in the right context. Similar to climbing a mountain, tactics one might employ at base camp can be counterproductive, if not fatal, near the summit. With our Crossroads Model, we have outlined some broad parameters and specific actions on what to do, and when, to greatly increase your chances of digital success.

A Final Chord

As we noted in the introduction, by 2020 we believe many managers will be asked two questions: Did you see the technical change coming? And, if so, what did you do about it? With this book, we have sought to help you answer those questions confidently and affirmatively. With a transition of this scale and complexity, much will change in the coming years. Ultimate success will require an open mind, perseverance, and courage. You have the power to choose whether this is a song of hope, or miles of bad road. This is true for your organization, your career, and, ultimately, your family, community, and society.

Notes

Chapter 1

1. http://online.wsj.com/article/SB100014240531119034809045765122509156 29460.html
2. http://propellerhealth.com/solutions/
3. "By 2025 the Second Economy will be as large as the 1995 physical economy." See W. Brian Arthur, Santa Fe Institute—*McKinsey Quarterly*, October 2011; www.mckinsey.com/insights/strategy/the_second_economy
4. Except where otherwise noted, all financial data is from S&P CapitalIQ. We looked at the maximum market capitalization in each year.
5. News Corp bought MySpace for $580 million in 2005 and sold it for $35 million in 2011. See www.npr.org/blogs/thetwo-way/2011/06/29/137509647/news-corp-takes-huge-loss-selling-myspace-for-35-million
6. HMV's market cap was about £10 million at the end of 2012. See www.retail-week.com/analysis-how-can-hmv-heal-its-trading-wounds/5044185.article
7. http://content.time.com/time/magazine/article/0,9171,2022624,00.html
8. www.industryweek-digital.com/industryweek/201302?pg=21#pg21
9. www.fastcompany.com/3005528/most-innovative-companies-mark-parker-nikes-digital-future

Chapter 2

1. http://newsroom.fb.com/Key-Facts
2. www.theatlanticwire.com/technology/2013/05/netflix-youtube-traffic/65210/
3. www.ericsson.com/res/docs/whitepapers/wp-50-billions.pdf and http://news.cnet.com/8301-13506_3-57377325-17/number-of-mobile-devices-to-hit-8-billion-by-2016-cisco-says/
4. http://en.wikipedia.org/wiki/Comparison_of_Android_devices and http://en.wikipedia.org/wiki/IPhone#Sales_and_profits
5. www.sciencedaily.com/releases/2013/05/130522085217.htm and www.forbes.com/sites/ciocentral/2013/02/04/big-data-big-hype/
6. http://en.wikipedia.org/wiki/Big_data
7. http://exabyte.bris.ac.uk/
8. www.emc.com/leadership/programs/digital-universe.htm
9. http://investor.pandora.com/phoenix.zhtml?c=227956&p=irol-newsArticle&ID=1845001&highlight=
10. www.forbes.com/sites/louiscolumbus/2012/11/08/cloud-computing-and-enterprise-software-forecast-update-2012/

Chapter 3

1. www.amazon.com/gp/betterizer/ref=pd_ys_sf_bzer_ad
2. http://en.wikipedia.org/wiki/Kevin_Ashton
3. http://newsroom.cisco.com/feature-content?type=webcontent&articleId=1208342
4. www.wired.com/gadgetlab/2011/10/nest_thermostat/
5. www.geoffshackelford.com/homepage/2013/8/30/look-out-foley-nike-patents-wearable-instruction-shirt.html
6. Roughly 25% of all heart failure patients are readmitted within 30 days due to complications and difficulty following challenging care regimens. Proteus is developing an ingestible chip—powered by gastric acid—to help ensure prescription compliance for multiple conditions. See www.proteus.com/future-products/therapeutic-areas/
7. For information on the GE aircraft engine Code Halo, see www.computerweekly.com/news/2240176561/Interview-with-GEs-head-of-software-William-Ruh Also see http://gigaom.com/2012/02/10/bits-meet-bite-check-out-the-connected-toothbrush/
8. www.tlnt.com/2013/02/26/how-google-is-using-people-analytics-to-completely-reinvent-hr/
9. http://en.wikipedia.org/wiki/Contextomy and www.chicagotribune.com/entertainment/movies/mmx-070209-movies-review-norbit,0,6004427.story

Chapter 4

1. www.gartner.com/newsroom/id/2610015
2. http://royal.pingdom.com/2013/01/16/internet-2012-in-numbers/
3. http://pewinternet.org/Infographics/2013/Broadband-and-smartphone-adoption.aspx
4. http://en.wikipedia.org/wiki/Moore's_law
5. www.livescience.com/18238-smart-clothing-wearable-gadgets.html
6. The First Warning System provides early breast cancer discovery by embedding sensor technology into clothing. See www.firstwarningsystems.com/
7. www.gereports.com/brilliant-iron/
8. Companies like Progressive (www.progressive.com/auto/snapshot-how-it-works/) and Allstate (www.allstate.com/drive-wise.aspx) are working to mature usage-based insurance models that connect prices to actual driving behavior tracked by proprietary devices.
9. http://blog.facebook.com/blog.php?post=2207967130
10. http://techcrunch.com/2006/09/06/facebook-users-revolt-facebook-replies/
11. www.insidefacebook.com/2008/08/19/mapping-facebooks-growth-over-time/
12. www.statisticbrain.com/facebook-statistics/
13. www.whatisedgerank.com/

14. http://lifehacker.com/5052851/information-overload-is-filter-failure-says-shirky and www.shirky.com/

15. www.youtube.com/watch?v=Y34JYb4NMLo

16. www.fidelityworldwideinvestment.com/middle-east/news-insight/21-century-themes/episode5.page

17. www.gizmag.com/go/7549/

18. http://gigaom.com/2013/07/25/at-netflix-big-data-can-affect-even-the-littlest-things/

19. William Goldman. *Adventures in the Screen Trade: A Personal View of Hollywood and Screenwriting.* New York: Warner Books, 1983, and http://en.wikipedia.org/wiki/William_Goldman

20. http://bgr.com/2013/07/18/netflix-original-series-emmy-nominations/

21. www.nytimes.com/2013/02/25/business/media/for-house-of-cards-using-big-data-to-guarantee-its-popularity.html?pagewanted=all&_r=0

22. HIPPO stands for the "highest paid person's opinion." It's not a compliment. See www.forbes.com/sites/derosetichy/2013/04/15/what-happens-when-a-hippo-runs-your-company/

23. www.ingentaconnect.com/content/ben/aps/2013/00000003/00000002/art00006

24. http://blogs.sap.com/innovation/industries/tooth-sensors-can-help-speed-weight-loss-fight-cavities-0498824

25. https://squareup.com/wallet

26. www.respondpowerrewards.com/

27. www.emc.com/collateral/emc-perspective/h11490-big-data-transforms-life-sciences-commercial-model-ep.pdf

28. www.worldcrunch.com/tech-science/take-back-control-of-your-personal-data-then-sell-it-to-highest-bidder/start-up-yes-profile-advertising-profile-internet/c4s11754/ and www.technologyreview.com/news/428046/a-dollar-for-your-data/

29. http://en.wikipedia.org/wiki/Zune

Chapter 5

1. This is based on our analysis of multiple industry reports.

2. http://readwrite.com/2013/09/30/how-big-the-internet-of-things-could-become#feed=/infrastructure&awesm=~omnisA2MfHCPe7

3. www.emc.com/leadership/programs/digital-universe.htm

4. Dan Woods, "The Naked Mainframe," Forbes.com, January 19, 2010, www.forbes.com/2010/01/18/mainframe-security-enterprise-technology-cio-network-woods.html

5. www.ieeeghn.org/wiki6/index.php/STARS:Rise_and_Fall_of_Minicomputers and http://en.wikipedia.org/wiki/Digital_Equipment_Corporation#PDP-11 and http://en.wikipedia.org/wiki/Exabyte

6. www.statisticbrain.com/computer-sales-statistics/ and
    www.historyofcomputercommunications.info/Overview/MarketResearch/2-
    ComputerTerminalSales68-88.html and http://highscalability.com/
    blog/2012/9/11/how-big-is-a-petabyte-exabyte-zettabyte-or-a-yottabyte.html

7. www.businessinsider.com/the-complete-history-of-computer-and-gadget-sales-in-
    one-elegant-chart-2012-1

8. www.reuters.com/article/2011/06/08/us-bigdata-idUSTRE75762Y20110608

9. www.theguardian.com/technology/blog/2012/jan/11/ces-2012-intel-keynote-
    otellini/

10. http://news.idg.no/cw/art.cfm?id=39345632-FC5F-F03F-1BFFF7B485F4BBE3

11. www.hindustantimes.com/technology/industrytrends/over-100-billion-mobile-
    apps-downloaded-in-2013/article1-1124695.aspx

12. www.inquisitr.com/328075/mobile-app-market-to-double-in-2012-reach-45-
    billion-annual-downloads/

13. See "Mobile Is the New Face of Engagement," by Forrester Research http://media
    .cms.bmc.com/documents/Mobile_Is_The_New_Face_Of.pdf

14. http://gigaom.com/mobile/did-you-hear-that-a-billion-smartphones-shipping-
    by-2016/

15. Matthew Shaer, "iPhone Sales Top 5 Million, But Miss Some Estimates," *The
    Christian Science Monitor*, September 24, 2012, www.csmonitor.com/Innovation/
    Horizons/2012/0924/iPhone-5-sales-top-5-million-but-miss-some-estimates

16. www.nbcnews.com/technology/technolog/android-market-catching-apple-app-
    numbers-118119

17. www.appbrain.com/stats/number-of-android-apps

18. See "Cisco Visual Networking Index Forecast Projects 18-Fold Growth in Global
    Mobile Internet Data Traffic From 2011 to 2016," Cisco, February 14, 2012,
    http://newsroom.cisco.com/press-release-content?articleId=668380

19. "The Internet of Things: Smart Houses, Smart Traffic, Smart Health," *Science
    Daily*, June 26, 2012, www.sciencedaily.com/releases/2012/06/120626065009
    .htm

20. http://scn.sap.com/people/richard.hirsch/blog/2012/02/15/sap-and-the-internet-
    of-things-or-why-the-business-web-will-be-critical-for-saps-future-ondemand-
    success

21. See "U.S. Newspaper Ad Revenue Down 27% in 2009: NAA,"
    Google, March 25, 2010, www.google.com/hostednews/afp/article/
    ALeqM5hhm0W0vYR79VIvsbUpQvDv_fegyQ

22. See "The State of the News Media 2012," The Pew Research Center, http://
    stateofthemedia.org/2012/newspapers-building-digital-revenues-proves-painfully-
    slow/newspapers-by-the-numbers/

23. http://en.wikipedia.org/wiki/Craigslist and CNET, May 22, 2009 and http://news.cnet.com/8301-1023_3-10247668-93.html

24. See company reports and "Wikipedia Statistics," http://en.wikipedia.org/wiki/Wikipedia:Statistics

Chapter 6

1. www.businessinsider.com/jim-chanos-on-how-value-stocks-decline-2012-12

2. www.pbig.ml.com/pwa/pages/Millennials-and-Money.aspx and http://thefinancialbrand.com/34480/millennials-desperate-better-fees-convenience/

3. www.healthx.com/global/resource-center/infographics/customer-satisfaction-with-health-insurance-sites/

4. www.progressive.com/progressive-insurance/history.aspx

5. http://en.wikipedia.org/wiki/PageRank

6. http://radar.oreilly.com/2007/04/why-google-is-offering-411-ser.html

7. http://tctechcrunch2011.files.wordpress.com/2013/02/itunes-downloads13b.png

8. http://en.wikipedia.org/wiki/Template:Facebook_growth#cite_ref-3

9. http://forwardthinking.pcmag.com/none/300368-marc-andreessen-explains-why-software-is-eating-the-world

Chapter 7

1. Data in this chapter is from a 2013 research study by Cognizant and Oxford Economics unless otherwise noted. Oxford Economics is one of the world's foremost independent global advisory firms, providing reports, forecasts, thought leadership, and analytical tools that cover some 190 countries, 100 industrial sectors, and over 2,600 cities.

2. See McKinsey Global Institute (2012) Big Data: The next frontier for innovation, competition and productivity; www.mckinsey.com/insights/business_technology/big_data_the_next_frontier_for_innovation

3. More specifically, our analysis estimated annual cost reductions of some $78 billion to U.S. healthcare payers and providers over the past financial year compared to McKinsey's estimate of $226 billion in potential savings. Revenue gains for U.S. healthcare payers and providers for the past financial year ($107 billion) were equivalent to those suggested by McKinsey ($107 billion per year).

4. www.tomdavenport.com/about/ and www.sas.com/resources/asset/IIA_NewWorldofBusinessAnalytics_March2010.pdf

5. www.cognizant.com/Futureofwork/Documents/dont-get-smacked.pdf

6. Unattributed quotes and data in this chapter are derived from our own research. Read the full study here: http://bit.ly/L13r5H

7. Taylorism is a business management system that emphasized granular work process breakdowns and task management. See www.britannica.com/EBchecked/topic/1387100/Taylorism

8. www.oxfordeconomics.com/Media/Default/Thought percent 20Leadership/global-talent-2021.pdf

9. www.nhtsa.gov/UA

10. www.fundinguniverse.com/company-histories/netflix-inc-history/

11. http://is.jrc.ec.europa.eu/pages/ISG/documents/FINALNewsreportwithcovers.pdf

Chapter 8

1. www.kpcb.com/insights/2012-internet-trends and www.forbes.com/sites/ericjackson/2012/12/10/mary-meeker-is-right-the-next-5-years-will-see-a-re-imagination-of-everything-including-the-venture-capital-industry/

2. www.theguardian.com/technology/2010/jun/23/iphone4-first-review-stephen-fry

3. www.ilounge.com/index.php/reviews/entry/nike-nike-fuelband/

4. www.philly.com/philly/blogs/trending/This-is-how-Netflix-reads-your-mind.html

5. http://wheels.blogs.nytimes.com/2012/12/04/can-lincoln-regain-its-relevance/

6. www.nytimes.com/2009/07/12/automobiles/12jaguar-xj.html?_r=0

7. www.autoguide.com/manufacturer/jaguar/2008-jaguar-xf-supercharged-988.html

8. www.nytimes.com/2008/05/04/automobiles/autosreviews/04jaguar-xf.html?pagewanted=print&_r=0

9. www.nytimes.com/2008/05/04/automobiles/autosreviews/04jaguar-xf.html

10. http://techcrunch.com/2013/03/27/idc-tablet-growth-2012-2017/

11. http://paidcontent.org/2012/08/30/amazon-says-kindle-fire-makes-up-22-of-u-s-tablet-sales/

12. http://mashable.com/2012/08/21/barnes-nobles-nook-sales-decline/

13. www.businessweek.com/articles/2013-07-25/the-end-barnes-and-noble-in-silicon-valley

14. http://the.echonest.com/solutions/

15. http://musicalidentity.echonest.com/post/53274129750/how-music-taste-predicts-movie-taste

16. http://notes.variogr.am/post/26869688460/how-well-does-music-predict-your-politics

17. www.noiseaddicts.com/2008/09/music-tastes-indicates-personality-study/ and http://urbantimes.co/2012/12/what-does-your-musical-preference-say-about-your-personality/, and http://hellobeautiful.com/1139465/is-there-a-correlation-between-music-taste-your-personality/

18. http://news.bbc.co.uk/2/hi/entertainment/5343598.stm and http://uspace.shef.ac.uk/servlet/JiveServlet/previewBody/53581-102-1-103169/North,%20Hargreaves.%20Lifestyle%20correlates%20of%20musical%20preference.pdf

19. http://mashable.com/2013/05/22/pandora-facebook-2/

20. See Google platform definition, http://en.wikipedia.org/wiki/Google_platform
21. Johann Wolfgang von Goethe, and R. Dillon Boylan, Novels and tales by Goethe: *Elective Affinities; The Sorrows of Werther; German Emigrants; The Good Women;* and *A Nouvelette* (London: H.G. Bohn, 1854).

Chapter 9

1. www.theatlantic.com/politics/archive/2013/06/all-the-infrastructure-a-tyrant-would-need-courtesy-of-bush-and-obama/276635/
2. According to Royal Pingdom (http://royal.pingdom.com/), a website performance and monitoring company.
3. www.cnn.com/2013/04/04/justice/craiglist-killer-death-sentence/
4. www.nbcnews.com/technology/aclu-digital-dragnet-ensnares-millions-innocent-drivers-6C10654018
5. http://www.startribune.com/local/minneapolis/166494646.html
6. http://www.csmonitor.com/USA/Latest-News-Wires/2013/0718/License-plate-scanners-have-allowed-police-to-log-location-and-movement-of-millions
7. www.cnn.com/2013/07/17/us/aclu-license-plates-readers/
8. www.pcworld.com/article/255920/liberating_your_data_from_google_and_what_that_really_means.html
9. www.patient.co.uk/doctor/fitness-to-drive
10. www.flhsmv.gov/forms/72190.pdf
11. www.bmj.com/content/313/7056/518
12. http://papers.ssrn.com/sol3/papers.cfm?abstract_id=1782267
13. www.pbs.org/wgbh/nova/body/hippocratic-oath-today.html
14. www.bizjournals.com/sanjose/news/2013/09/23/clear-history-minors-in-calif-will.html

Chapter 10

1. www.wirearchy.com
2. http://quoteinvestigator.com/2013/06/10/showing-up/
3. www.technologyreview.com/news/422784/qa-the-experimenter/
4. www.kaushik.net/avinash/
5. www.ted.com/talks/juan_enriquez_how_to_think_about_digital_tattoos.htm

Chapter 11

1. http://hbr.org/2003/05/it-doesnt-matter/ar/1
2. Baghai, Mehrdad, Stephen Coley, and David White. *The Alchemy of Growth*, London: Orion Business Books, 1999.
3. Christensen, Clayton M., *The Innovator's Dilemma*, Boston, Mass.: Harvard Business School Press, 1997.

4. Diagram based on The Three Horizon Model from McKinsey & Company. See www.mckinsey.com/insights/strategy/enduring_ideas_the_three_horizons_of_ growth

5. Minimum Viable Product and Lean innovation ideas are based on work by Eric Ries. See Ries, Eric. *The Lean Startup*. New York: Crown Business, 2011.

6. www.forbes.com/sites/lisaarthur/2012/02/08/five-years-from-now-cmos-will-spend-more-on-it-than-cios-do/

Chapter 12

1. Stephen Ezell, "The State of Innovation in the States," Information Technology Innovation Foundation, 2012, http://www2.itif.org/2012-state-innovation-states.pdf

2. www.rjgeorge.com/archives/32

3. See Roberto Venturini, "Innovation and Competition: Introducing Network Externalities," Université Libre de Bruxelles, 2012.

4. www.kauffman.org/what-we-do/research/2009/08/the-economic-future-just-happened

5. Michael E. Porter, *Competitive Advantage: Creating and Sustaining Superior Performance*. New York: Free Press, 1985.

6. Dinesh Pratap Singh's visualization for Porter's Value Chain, see http://en.wikipedia.org/wiki/File:Porter_Value_Chain.png

7. Geoffrey Moore, author, educator, and a leading mind in enterprise technology, coined the term "moments of engagement" to describe the intersection—or collision—among technologies, companies, and consumers. See http://blogs.sap .com/innovation/innovation/geoffrey-moore-we-need-a-revolution-of-enterprise-it-08973

8. See "The Next Network," www.siemens.com/innovation/apps/pof_microsite/_ pof-fall-2012/_html_en/m2m.html

9. www.bmw.com/com/en/insights/technology/technology_guide/articles/ onboard_diagnosis.html

10. www.gtnexus.com/

11. http://ww1.jeppesen.com/aviation/mobile-efb/index.jsp and http://ww1 .jeppesen.com/company/newsroom/articles.jsp?newsURL=news/newsroom/2013/ Delta_Surface2EFB_NR.jsp

Chapter 13

1. This is not much of an exaggeration. Employers and consumers consistently and passionately express extreme dissatisfaction with healthcare insurers. See www.jdpower.com/content/press-release/aetaQ91/2013-employer-health-plan-study.htm and www.gallup.com/poll/164093/images-banking-real-estate-making-comeback.aspx

Chapter 14

1. http://tctechcrunch2011.files.wordpress.com/2013/02/itunes-downloads13b.png
2. http://en.wikipedia.org/wiki/Template:Facebook_growth#cite_ref-3
3. http://en.wikipedia.org/wiki/Facebook
4. http://en.wikipedia.org/wiki/Twitter
5. http://betabeat.com/2012/02/nike-fuelband-apple-sold-out-02232012/
6. http://en.wikipedia.org/wiki/The_Singularity_Is_Near
7. www.aiqsmartclothing.com/ and www.medgadget.com/2013/09/aiqs-bioman-biomonitoring-shirt-and-other-smart-clothing-technology.html
8. http://en.wikipedia.org/wiki/Jack_Dorsey and www.cbsnews.com/video/watch/?id=50143017n and www.npr.org/2012/02/08/145470844/revolution-2-0-how-social-media-toppled-a-dictator
9. www.bristol.ac.uk/cubec/portal/pr1.pdf

Photo Credits

Page 8: Digital DNA. Sergey Nivens | Shutterstock

Page 39: Amplifier. Denyshutter | Thinkstock

Page 40: Hand on tablet. Peshkova | Shutterstock

Page 49: Container ship. Stewart Sutton | Digital Vision | Getty Images

Page 99: Money pile. Serg Dibrova | Shutterstock

Page 101: Running shoes. Warren Goldswain | Shutterstock

Page 116: Hiker. Dudarev Mikhail | Shutterstock

Page 121: Mobile check-in app. Ryccio | iStock Vendors | Getty Images

Page 122: License plate camera. ELSAG

Page 144: Security camera. Blazej Lyjak | Shutterstock

Page 175: Urban crossroads. Zoonar | Thinkstock

Page 192: Storm cloud. Zastolskiy Victor | Shutterstock

Index